D0016805

# HYGGE

# HYGGE

a celebration of simple pleasures.
living the danish way

## charlotte abrahams

TRAPEZE

First published in Great Britain in 2016 by Trapeze,
an imprint of The Orion Publishing Group Ltd
Carmelite House, 50 Victoria Embankment,
London EC4Y 0DZ

An Hachette UK company

1 3 5 7 9 10 8 6 4 2

Copyright © Charlotte Abrahams 2016

The moral right of Charlotte Abrahams to be identified as the author of this work has been asserted in accordance with the Copyright, Designs and Patents Act of 1988.

All rights reserved. No part of this publication may be reproduced, stored in a retrieval system, or transmitted in any form or by any means, electronic, mechanical, photocopying, recording, or otherwise, without the prior permission of both the copyright owner and the above publisher of this book.

PICTURE CREDITS:

Page 12: Fritz Hansen; Page 24: Getty; Page 40-41: Alamy; Page 47: Faaborg Chair by Carl Hansen & Søn PR photo; Page 49: Louis Poulsen PH Artichoke designed by Poul Henningsen at Silver Mountain, Senzoku Gakuen College Of Music; Page 50: Louis Poulsen PH5 pendant light designed by Poul Henningsen; Page 53: Carl Hansen & Son CH24 Wishbone chair designed by Hans J Wegner; Page 54: Carl Hansen & Son CH29 Sawbuck chair designed by Hans J Wegner; Page 55: Carl Hansen & Son CH07 Shell chair designed by Hans J Wegner; Page 57: House of FinnJuhl TM; Page 58: House of FinnJuhl TM; Page 61: Alamy; Page 66: Louis Poulsen PH Artichoke designed by Poul Henningsen at Silver Mountain, Senzoku Gakuen College Of Music; Page 69: Alamy; Page 70: Alamy; Page 72: LE KLINT; Page 74: House of FinnJuhl TM; Page 76: Getty; Page 82: Getty; Page 94: Shutterstock/AS Food Studio; Page 104: Ty Strange; Page 116: Getty; Page 130-1: Getty; Page 134: Getty; Page 137: Getty; Page 138: Getty; Page 141: Getty; Page 152: Alamy; Page 164: Getty; Page 176: Alamy; Page 182: Getty; Page 194-5: Shutterstock/KN; Page 198: Getty; Page 203: Getty; Page 204: Getty; Page 208: Getty; Page 211: Shutterstock/ThomsonD

A CIP catalogue record for this book is available from the British Library.

ISBN (Hardback) 978 1 4091 6759 4
ISBN (Export Trade Paperback) 978 1 4091 6800 3

Printed in Italy

www.orionbooks.co.uk

MIX
Paper from
responsible sources
FSC
www.fsc.org     FSC® C015829

For George and Hamish, with my love always

What is this life if, full of care,

We have no time to stand and stare.

No time to stand beneath the boughs

And stare as long as sheep or cows.

No time to see, when woods we pass,

Where squirrels hide their nuts in grass.

No time to see, in broad daylight,

Streams full of stars, like skies at night.

No time to turn at Beauty's glance,

And watch her feet, how they can dance.

No time to wait till her mouth can

Enrich that smile her eyes began.

A poor life this if, full of care,

We have no time to stand and stare.

'Leisure', William Henry Davies

# CONTENTS

'*For me, hygge is about taking pleasure in the small things in life: having a cup of coffee in the afternoon; being woken by the cat's gentle purring; walking in the sunshine or spending time with loved ones. Hygge is about enjoying the moment and feeling content in that moment. It's about taking an active part in your own enjoyment – you're not just doing it to relax or pass the time, but as a way of being present*'

# INTRODUCTION

You will already have guessed from my name that I am not Danish. What I should also make clear before we begin is that I have never lived in Denmark, and the only Danish people I know are those I met during my research for this book. I have been to Copenhagen and, while I found both the city and its inhabitants to be friendly, cultured and aesthetically pleasing, I was taken aback by the climate. Copenhagen in February is cold and damp – like the UK, only more so. (It is on the same latitude as Glasgow and, soft southerner that I am, I have never been tempted to go there in winter.) A sleet-filled wind blew up the waterways all day, every day, and settled into my bones. The experience was enough to convince me that, no matter how liveable a capital it is reputed to be, I could not possibly make my home there.

Why, then, am I writing a book about something so profoundly Danish as hygge? Let me explain.

I first came across the term a couple of years ago in a glossy interiors magazine. The caption told me that it is the Danish word for 'turning your home into a cosy haven to nurture you through the dark winters'. The pictures showed slubby woollen blankets, enveloping cushions, lots of perfectly formed Danish mid-century furniture and an abundance of candles. It was November. In my particular corner of Gloucestershire it was, once again, mizzling gently, day barely distinguishable from night and, like many of us who work from home, I was counting the minutes before I could decently put the heating on. Against this background, the hygge aesthetic looked very alluring indeed, and I made a note to buy myself a sofa blanket as soon as the next writing commission came through.

Some weeks later I saw the word again and, curious about where it had come from, I typed it into Google. I discovered that, while cosy throws and candles do indeed play a part (the Danes burn more candles per head of population than any other country in Europe, apparently), hygge is far more than an uber-fashionable fad for cold homeworkers and fans of Scandi chic. Pronounced 'hoo-ga', the term comes from the Norwegian word for 'well-being' and is believed to be loosely connected to the English word 'hug', an obsolete meaning of which is, according to the *Oxford English Dictionary*, 'to cherish oneself; to makes oneself snug'.

Very little has been written about the origins of hygge, but it is generally understood to have first appeared in Denmark in the eighteenth century. The reasons why the concept emerged at that time are undocumented, as far as I can tell, but the timing is interesting.

The beginning of the eighteenth century saw Denmark contract as it lost territories following the Great Northern War of 1700–21; the Danes may have defeated their enemy Sweden, but they still had to give back Swedish Pomerania, and the country never regained control of the Eastern Provinces. One of the consequences of such large-scale downsizing was that this once outward-looking nation began to turn its attention inwards. Nationalism thrived – a law was passed banning foreigners from holding government posts – along with pride in the uniqueness of the language.

Most imported words cross borders unnoticed and seep unconsciously into another nation's vocabulary, but Susanne Nilsson, whose Danish-language course at Morley College in London includes a brief study of hygge, told me that the Danes' adoption of the word 'hygge' was a studiedly deliberate attempt to create something which they could proudly call their own. Linguistically, they took it from the Norwegians as a noun and then embellished it, turning it into a verb and adding an adjectival form (hyggelig/hyggeligt/hyggelige – the difference between each is explained in the quick guide to hygge grammar on page 218) for good measure.

As for what it meant, then as now hygge had a multiplicity of meanings, ranging from a way of describing cosy surroundings to the relaxing experience of pleasant conversation with friends. But essentially hygge was conceived as a concept centred on refuge; on the home as a comforting sanctuary from the outside world and a safe place to withdraw to with your loved ones. The climate no doubt had a role to play (snuggling up in a warm room with your nearest and dearest is a good way to break the cold, dark monotony of a Danish winter after all), but it seems likely that this desire to pull up the metaphorical drawbridge is also linked to the inward-facing attitude of eighteenth-century Denmark.

Today, hygge is so firmly ingrained into Danish life that it has become part of what it is to be a Dane. The idea that a space must cocoon its occupants is still important, as is spending time with family and friends, but there are many other elements, too. Contemporary hygge calls for total immersion in the moment, for example; it is about gentle pleasure, and it acknowledges that we need to pay attention to our well-being. The anthropologist Judith Friedman Hansen gives an eloquent description of the spirit of hygge in her book *We are a Little Land: Cultural Assumptions in Danish Everyday Life*. She writes that it is widely understood to mean 'being in a state of pleasant well-being and security, with a relaxed frame of mind and open enjoyment of the immediate situation in all its small pleasures'.[1] The Danes practise hygge consciously – 'kan du hygge dig' (roughly meaning 'what a hyggelig time we had'), friends will say to each other by way of goodbye at the end of an evening – and its presence in daily life is taken for granted.

I didn't know much about Denmark when I started looking into hygge, but the one thing I did know was that the Danes have an enviable quality of life, and top the world happiness charts with a consistency that those of us living in less happy nations can find irksome. I had always assumed this abundance of happiness was a result of their belief in high taxes as fair exchange for health, education and welfare systems which meet peoples' needs. Having discovered that one of Denmark's most prevalent cultural traditions is based on cherishing, snugness and the enjoyment of small pleasures, however, I began to reassess.

My initial idea was to write a book about the role hygge plays in Denmark's much-publicised sense of positive well-being; does their excellent work–life balance (they work some of the shortest hours of any nation in the world), for example, have anything to do with the fact that spending time with friends and family is considered to be very hyggelig indeed? But the more I thought about it, the more I kept coming back to that word 'cherish'. I was struck by what a lovely word it is, and how underused. I couldn't remember the last time I had consciously cherished anyone, so the idea of a lifestyle philosophy that puts cherishing family and friends and, even more interestingly, oneself at its centre fascinated me. I decided to make my research a bit more personal and see what living a more hyggelig life could do for me.

This is out of character; I don't believe that we should try to reinvent ourselves and I am generally dismissive of lifestyle philosophies, particularly as so many of those on offer today seem to be rooted in denial. Denial is a nasty, bad-tempered notion that stems from a belief that pleasure is in some way sinful and that we would all be better people with less of it in our lives. (Banning fat, sugar, wheat and clothes you haven't worn in the last six months is the twenty-first century equivalent of donning a hair shirt.) However, I have recently emerged from a decade of turmoil that sees me approaching my fiftieth birthday as a twice-divorced soon-to-be-empty-nester, and I have promised myself, as well as my friends and my family, that I will deal with turning fifty with more serenity than I managed when I hit forty. (It won't be difficult because I did not manage forty. I crashed into it and it exploded around me as I uprooted my life, driven by the fear that I would die before I had – what? Done more? Who knows, but I felt I was stagnating and running out of time.) I am therefore at a Significant Moment; if ever there was a time for a bit of reappraisal, then I suppose that time is now.

Hygge appealed because it is not about denial; it is generous of spirit. There are no manuals or mantras, no prescriptive lists of things you must, or must not, do. It is simply about taking the occasional break from life and allowing yourself to enjoy the moment. Hygge encourages us to take pleasure in the modest, the mundane and the familiar. It is a celebration of the everyday, and it prioritises experiences over things. Talking with a friend by an open fire is hyggelig; cooking supper with your children is hyggelig; running through beech woods in the early-morning mist is hyggelig; a large glass of wine in front of the telly is hyggelig.

I am aware that choosing to embrace hygge could be seen as the choice of a middle-aged woman searching for a life philosophy but who is too fond of cake for clean living and more interested in interior design than meditation. Not to mention tired of being advised to employ a lifestyle coach to help Maximise Her Potential. Well, guilty as charged. But, while I accept that the soft, fluffy bits of hygge – the comforting food, the candles, the well-designed furniture – did play a part in my decision, what really piqued my interest was the discovery that hygge prioritises self-kindness and quiet contentment.

I have misunderstood contentment. For years I mixed it up with complacency, with a slippered sitting back that I still find terrifying, but – and I know this is to do with the onset of middle age – I am coming to realise that contentment is the foundation on which the infinitely more exciting, high-octane sort of happiness rests. Without contentment there are only baubles.

Self-kindness is underrated, too. We might tell our children that they should accept and love who they are, but in reality we are a society that endlessly pushes self-improvement. At the root of every diet book and lifestyle guide is the idea that we could be better people if only we put the effort in. (And the root of *that* idea grows out of a very unpleasant seed indeed; one that spreads the message that we are not quite good enough as we are.) I am sure some people do stick to the rules of their chosen diet or new way of living and emerge enriched, but most of us give up and return to our old habits feeling that we have failed. Feeling that we have failed is a fast route to discontent.

So what exactly have I done? The changes to my life have been modest, since it would have been most unhyggelig to do anything too radical – hygge is an understated, low-key concept after all, which is another of its charms. I was told that the average Dane aims to do at least two or three hyggelige things each week: perhaps a picnic with friends, an evening alone watching Nordic Noir under a blanket and an afternoon baking ginger biscuits with the kids. I have tried to follow suit, concentrating on striking an even balance between doing hygge with my friends and family and hygging by myself. I have also made some minor adjustments to my interior decor in an attempt to increase the 'cosy rating' of my home.

The biggest change, however, has been not in what I have done, but the way in which I have done it. If there are any hygge rules, then the most fundamental is the one about presence: for something to be hyggelig, everyone involved must be fully committed to the moment. I am a multitasking woman; focusing on one thing does not come naturally to me.

As for whether I have succeeded, all I can say is that I have tried my best. This book is an account of my experiment in hyggelig living, intertwined with my personal reflections on hygge as a cultural phenomenon and the role it has played in making Denmark such a happy country. I have also included a number of first-hand descriptions of hygge which you will find scattered throughout the book. There are 'how to' sections, too, which I know, strictly speaking, goes against the non-prescriptive spirit of hygge. In my defence, I will say that these sections are not lists of rules; rather collections of well-meant suggestions based on my own experience. Do with them as you wish. But above all, what follows here is an exploration of contentment: what it is, why it is important and whether allowing ourselves to raise the white flag from time to time and take a moment to celebrate simple pleasures can help us to achieve it.

*'What does hygge mean to me? Home-cooked food enjoyed with good friends at a pretty table; curling up with a book under a throw with hot chocolate; a room with flowers and candles and low lighting; an evening in front of an open fire, talking; and Saturday lunch out with my husband – a tradition we have had ever since we met almost forty years ago'*

# HYGGE
# BY DESIGN

# EVEN THE AIRPORT
# HAS PARQUET FLOORS

You can tell a lot about a country from its airports. I flew into Beijing at the height of the bird flu scare and was marched through an electronic body thermometer before I had even presented my passport. On a July night in Chania, Crete, on the other hand, my fellow passengers and I waited at baggage reclaim for almost an hour as cases emerged sporadically through the plastic strips, the pauses in their appearance on the conveyor belt suspiciously consistent with the length of a handler's fag break.

Copenhagen airport has parquet floors.

Wheeling my suitcase across this smooth, quiet and soul-warming floor as I made my way to the exit, I was reminded of an article I'd read in *DANISH*™, an online magazine published by the Danish Design and Architecture Initiative. 'In Denmark, good design and great architecture are not just for the select few,' it stated. 'They are everywhere you go, surrounding our children in kindergarten, hospital patients, as well as tourists who are exploring our cities. Everybody benefits from well-executed solutions, objects and systems that are functional and beautiful.'[1] I was indeed benefiting, I thought. The modest chicness and surprising comfort of this airport was soothing spirits ruffled by the too-cramped, too-orange interior of an easyJet Airbus.

I am a design journalist, and I was aware that my physical environment influenced my state of mind long before I ever set foot in Copenhagen. I would spend hours as a child rearranging my bedroom to reflect the mood of that particular moment – heaps of ethnic cushions and joss sticks alternated with accessory-free austerity as I moved from sociable hippy chic to intense misunderstood loner. These days my home remains fairly constant, but buildings erected with no imagination, sensitivity or thought make me rather depressed, and I am irritated by objects that neither work nor please the eye, or are simply too full of their own importance. I also adjust hotel rooms to suit my personal aesthetic.

Once, accommodated in a bed and breakfast on a riding weekend in the Black Mountains of Wales, I was forced to hide the riotously floral quilt on top of the wardrobe and turn its matching duvet cover inside out in an attempt to fade colours and diminish an offbeat pattern that jangled my nerves. My elderly Polish host was not pleased by this disruption to what she considered a tastefully co-ordinated and cheerful scheme. She asked me what I did. When I told her, her tight lips cast doubt on my suitability for my chosen profession.

Beauty is indeed in the eye of the beholder, but we all fare better in surroundings that we think beautiful. I am aware that I am probably at the extreme end of the spectrum, but I do believe that we are all affected to some extent by the quality of our physical environment and the objects we interact with every day. As the philosopher Alain de Botton writes in his book *The Architecture of Happiness*, 'Taking architecture seriously requires that we open ourselves to the idea that we are affected by our surroundings . . . It means conceding that we are inconveniently vulnerable to the colour of our wallpaper.'[2]

It is a view echoed by Anthony Seldon, biographer and Vice-Chancellor of Buckingham University, who is perhaps best known as the headmaster who introduced well-being classes to Wellington

College. In his book *Beyond Happiness*, Seldon writes: 'The environ-ments we inhabit – our living rooms, bedrooms and offices, our back yards and gardens – are outer manifestations of our inner minds . . . Make a commitment to ensure that your environment remains in line with your ideals. Doing so will bring you happiness, because you will be in harmony with your environment, because that environment is in harmony with you.'[3]

You don't have to go to Denmark to realise that this is something the Danes understand. You can see the value they place on aesthetics and functionality in the quietly beautiful furniture they export to design stores all over the world. It is evident in the pieces produced by companies such as Carl Hansen & Søn, Fritz Hansen, Louis Poulsen and Fredericia, which were founded in the first half of the twentieth century (the period that gave birth to the Danish Modern movement and which is widely regarded as the golden age of Danish design), and who now combine re-editions of mid-century classics with new collections. It is there in work being made by young brands, too. HAY, DK3 and Design by Dane, to name just three, are all proudly bringing together the best of the past with the best of the present.

But if you do go, it is immediately obvious that the author of that piece in *DANISH™* was not exaggerating: the Danes really do believe that design can be used to improve the quality of people's lives, and the effect of that belief permeates far beyond the rarefied walls of the design establishment. As David Obel Rosenkvist, Brand Manager for lighting company Louis Poulsen explained to me, 'Design is a national sport in Denmark. We have all been surrounded by good design since childhood, so we understand that design impacts on human life.' It came as no surprise to me to discover that Denmark was the first country in the world to implement a defined design policy and, while it is true that political support for design has ebbed and flowed since that historic decision in 1997, in 2010 design was included in a government platform that set out the country's political vision and strategy for the coming decade.

∧∨∧

We had caught an early-morning flight to Copenhagen, so we were feeling the effects of too short a night by the time we arrived in the city centre. Our first thought was lunch and, too tired and hungry to go in search of anywhere special, we simply walked into a small neighbourhood sandwich bar a few feet away from our hotel. As I ordered my herring smørrebrød, I noticed that there was a Poul Henningsen pendant light hanging over the chipped Formica counter. Poul Henningsen is one of the great names of Danish Modern, a man who devoted his life to studying how he could bring comfort and ambience to the electrified light bulb, and whose solution was light-diffusing layered shades. His designs have become classics. In the United Kingdom they are the preserve of the wealthy design cognoscenti; in Copenhagen they are ubiquitous. In the UK a café like this one would no doubt have been lit by a strip light, and its harsh glare would have hurried us through our lunch. Here, comforted by the soft atmospheric light of the PH 2/1, we took our time.

Refreshed, we walked across the Knippelsbro Bridge to the Black Diamond Library. This glass-fronted extension to the old Royal Library, designed by the architects Schmidt Hammer Lassen, manages to be both visually arresting and modest thanks to generous expanses of black glass which reflect the stretch of water the building stands beside. We then wandered through the city centre and into the

Radisson Blu Royal Hotel Copenhagen – or the SAS Hotel as it was originally known. Designed inside and out by Arne Jacobsen, another star of Danish Modern, the lobby still boasts welcoming clusters of his womb-like Egg chairs. We finished our day with an early supper at Restaurant Kanalen, drawn in off the dark and sleet-soaked streets by the welcoming glow of its candlelit interior.

Lying in bed later, my boyfriend asked me whether I had seen any examples of hygge. I realised that, while we had eaten in a candlelit restaurant and seen plenty of cafés with cosy-looking blankets thrown over their outdoor chairs, we hadn't come across many places that would have made it into a magazine feature about hyggelige interiors. What we had experienced, though, from the moment we arrived at the airport terminal, was a great deal of human-centred design. As I thought about our day my overriding feeling was that, despite the truly terrible weather, this was a very pleasant and comfortable city to be in. A hyggelig city, you could say.

The thought made me wonder whether hygge had played a part in the formation of Denmark's design culture. It hadn't occurred to me before, but now that I was here in the capital city, I could certainly see plenty of connections. Hygge is a concept based around comfort, relaxation and the enjoyment of simple pleasures. Danish design is characterised by its modest good looks, its quiet functionality, its human warmth and its democratic accessibility (at least in theory: the mid-century classics are pricey now, but they were originally designed to be available to all). Hygge prioritises well-being; Danish design rests on a humanistic approach, and both are so embedded in the culture that they have become part of Danish identity.

Denmark's aesthetic reputation centres on the Danish Modern movement, which flourished during the middle years of the last century (roughly 1930–70), and established this small Northern European country as a design superpower. 'It is extraordinary that a relatively undeveloped country with no significant mining resources, but with a fine tradition of craftsmanship, suddenly in the middle of the twentieth century takes a leading position as a design nation,' Nicolai de Gier, Associate Professor, Architect MAA and Head of the Furniture Programme at the Danish Design School, told me.

Danish Modern didn't spring fully formed from a vacuum. It grew out of that tradition of quality craftsmanship coupled with the belief that, as David McFadden puts it in his book *Scandinavian Modern Design, 1880–1980*, 'to be significant, design must be an outgrowth of the fundamental values of society, and that the role of the artist/craftsman is to manifest such values through the creative process.'[4]

The belief that design could influence social progress which still holds fast today began with the Arts and Crafts movement in the late 1800s, but it really took hold in the 1920s. The idea of social democracy was gaining ground right across Scandinavia at the time and, in 1924, the Social Democratic Party swept to power in Denmark. Their goal was social progress, and the Party believed that good design had an important role to play.

The craft tradition is much older, dating back at least as far as the sixteenth century and the formation of the Danish Cabinet Maker's Guild in 1554. A couple of centuries later, two more state-supported craft organisations were launched: first the Royal Danish Academy of Arts, which was established to teach apprentice craftsmen (and they were men in those days) how to draw and then, shortly after, the Danish Furniture Stores. As well as selling work by the Academy of Arts-trained makers, the Stores provided wood, workshops, funds and valuable contacts with designers. Thus nurtured, the cabinetmaking industry thrived.

And so it continued to do, right through the industrial revolution and on into the twentieth century. While other nations rushed to pin their futures to the brave new machines, Denmark took industrialisation slowly and held on to its traditions. As David Ryan (retired Curator of Design, Minneapolis Institute of Art) writes in his essay 'Scandinavian Moderne: 1900–1960', 'faith in the importance of tradition as a foundation for innovation lay at the root of [the Danes'] attempt to fuse the work of the hand with that of the machine'.[5]

Out of this landscape came Kaare Klint, founder, in 1924, of the Royal Academy of Architecture (the institution which trained most of the movement's great names) and the undisputed father of Danish Modern. Klint was a product of the cabinetmaking tradition, a man who knew his design history and his dovetail joints. But he also recognised that Danish furniture was no longer meeting the needs of consumers, so he set out to change things. He began with a series of anthropological studies. He looked at what people stored, how they sat on their chairs and how they interacted with their tables and desks, and combined this research with careful analyses of furniture from the past. The result was a new style of furniture. Spare in form, it broke with the excesses of Victoriana; human in function, it was a softer and more comfortable version of the 'living machine' approach to Modernism that was being proposed by the Bauhaus.

Klint was followed by Børge Mogensen, a man who believed that furniture's main duty was to help people live more comfortable, efficient lives, and he criticised designers who 'by the force of the devil, try to adapt the human to the furniture'. Mogensen was so committed to functionality that his design for built-in storage units was based on detailed studies into the precise measurements of common objects such as shirts and cutlery.

Other key figures of the period were Finn Juhl, Hans Wegner, Arne Jacobsen and Nanna Ditzel, the movement's only woman. Some pushed the technological boundaries more than others – Jacobsen, for example, experimented with new materials such as fibreglass – but all shared the idea that good design should be quietly beautiful, fit for purpose and available to all. (In the early 1940s, Børge Mogensen and Hans Wegner designed a range called 'The People's Collection' under a programme initiated by the co-operative organisation FBD to provide 'modern, functional, useful furniture that would be affordable for all social classes'.)

The weather influenced these designers too – Denmark is a country where it is cold and dark for half of the year. The Danes may be famous for keeping stoic and carrying on – 'there's no such thing as bad weather, just the wrong clothes' the homily goes (I soon discovered that Converse sneakers in February are the wrong clothes) – but the weather in Denmark is hostile and it has fostered an appreciation of design that comforts and warms.

Much of the work the mid-century designers and architects created is still in use today. Jacobsen's Ant, Swan and Egg chairs, Henningsen's PH series of lights, Wegner's Wishbone chair are design classics in the best sense of the term – not confined to museums (although they are there), but in daily use in offices, public institutions and homes around the world and, as I discovered, so common a sight in Copenhagen that they are taken for granted. We sat on Wegner's Wishbone chairs at Restaurant Kanalen, Jacobsen's Series 7 chair in the Louisiana Museum Café and stood beneath more Poul Henningsen lights in the bookshop of the Charlottenborg Palace. These designs have endured because they marry faultless function with pleasing form and a recognition that design should, first and foremost, fulfil the human need for comfort. As Wegner said, 'a chair isn't just a piece of furniture but a work of art for the human form'.

It seems obvious; but Danish Modern was rare in terms of its human focus. Compare Finn Juhl with the great French Modernist Le Corbusier, for example. Le Corbusier advocated machines for living in. 'Home life today is being paralysed by the deplorable notion that we must have furniture,' he told his client Madame Savoye when she expressed a desire for an armchair and two sofas in her new sitting room. 'This notion should be rooted out and replaced by that of equipment.' The villa was – and still is – extraordinarily beautiful, a white box of reinforced concrete floating on stilts; a thing so perfect that it had to rise above the earth. It remains one of Modernism's finest buildings from an aesthetic perspective, but as a home it was a failure. The flat roof, much praised by Le Corbusier's fellow architects, leaked so badly that the Savoyes' young son contracted a chest infection and in 1937, a mere eight years after it was finished, his mother declared the house to be uninhabitable.

Finn Juhl's house, completed in 1947, was home to the Danish architect and designer until his death in 1989. Juhl is one of Danish Modern's biggest stars, and this L-shaped bungalow is an eloquent expression both of the style and of his belief that houses should be designed from the inside out – first the furniture, then the rooms and finally the facade. Modest, almost ordinary viewed alongside the Villa Savoye, the house nevertheless seduces as you walk around it. (It is now open to the public as part of the Ordrupgaard Museum a few kilometres north of Copenhagen.) There are full-length windows and scrubbed wooden floors, and the open-plan rooms are built around furniture designed for comfort and joy. ('It is fundamental that the furniture is practical,' Juhl wrote in 1982. 'Chairs are not designed to look at, but to sit on. But of course, it makes you happy if they are also worth looking at.') The mostly white walls are brightened by blocks of colour that speak of summer – a yellow ceiling, some grass-green upholstery, a sky-blue band around the bed. It is light and spare and as free from unnecessary ornamentation as all self-respecting Modernist houses must be, but it also feels like a house that could accommodate life as it is actually lived. Like a home.

Le Corbusier is still admired (I for one am awed by the purity of his architecture, moved by the stillness of his buildings), but the style of living he advocated has since been discredited. He drew plans of skyscraper cities standing tall in green spaces, cities rid of overcrowding and urban sprawl, but the utopian high-rise cities of his dreams, where 2,700 people shared a single front door and walked in parks made possible by building up rather than out, were realised as dystopian banlieues. Estates of bleak concrete tower blocks stripped of all sense of humanity left their inhabitants isolated from the city below. The kind of housing that, in 2016, former British Prime Minister David Cameron pledged to demolish, claiming that these 'brutal' tower blocks 'trap people in poverty' and are 'a gift to criminals and drug dealers'.

Danish Modern, on the other hand, remains an international byword for exemplary design. I don't know whether my idea that hygge has influenced the country's design culture is a view that is widely shared in Denmark itself, but my unscientific researches do suggest that I am not an entirely lone voice. Knud Erik Hansen, Chief Executive Officer of furniture brand Carl Hansen & Søn, told me that he could see strong links between Danish designers' use of natural materials and rounded forms and hygge's focus on comfort and safety, while Nicolai de Gier of the Danish Design School said,

'I am not the one that will say that hygge is the father of all, but I think it is intertwined with many aspects of the development of Danish design.'

For me, looking in from the outside, the links are clear. Hygge celebrates comfort, warmth and gentle, understated pleasure. Danish design focuses on making the user comfortable; it prioritises warming, natural materials and is characterised by its quiet, modest beauty. It is, Nicolai de Gier explained to me, 'rounded off by an ability to customise the ordinary and mundane, resulting in a refinery that gives the furniture a special characteristic. The ordinary becomes extraordinary.' These sensibilities are very similar and, in my opinion, all stem from a central belief that personal well-being is a matter worthy of serious attention.

# HOME IS WHERE THE HYGGE IS

'Wherever I lay my hat, that's my home,' sang Paul Young in 1983. I thought the idea rather romantic back then, but these days I'm with Dorothy: there really is no place quite like home.

It turns out that the Kansas girl in the red shoes was channelling hygge and its celebration of home, both as a physical building that protects and shelters its inhabitants from the outside world and as an idealised concept. This is hardly unique to the Danes – the cavemen grouped around their fires understood it, and you have only to look at the images of the insides of the tents refugees are currently being forced to live in to see the instinct to make a home in action – but it finds a particularly eloquent expression in hygge. In his paper 'Money Can't Buy Me Hygge', the Danish-Swedish anthropologist Jeppe Trolle Linnet cites references to the word's meaning in eighteenth-century Norwegian. They all centre on connotations such as 'the experience of comfort in one's home' and 'safe habitat'.[6]

I moved into my current home in February 2014 on the fourth anniversary of my second marriage. An uncelebrated anniversary, since the marriage was by then over bar the paperwork. The previous owners and I had exchanged contracts a month earlier, on my forty-sixth birthday (so much symbolism is a lot for one little bungalow, but I was keen to mark the milestones of my new life), and I had spent the intervening weeks decorating. I loathe DIY, and am prone to the kind of slapdash handiwork that leads to quick deterioration. I do not sand woodwork, which means that the new paint flakes.

I can't be bothered with lining paper. But I enjoyed making this house my own.

My decision to buy was based on the south-facing view, the presence of a hexagonal hut in the garden which I planned to use as an office, its well-maintained walls and the fact that I could afford it. I was also seduced by the sliding doors opening on to the deck, which suggested an indoor-outdoor California lifestyle (despite the geographical impossibility of such a thing), and the presence of peonies in the garden. But the real reason that I was – and have remained – so enamoured by this place had nothing to do with decking or flowers or walls that don't let the rain in. Physically, this 1960s bungalow is rather ugly, a sore thumb in a charming Cotswold village of honey-coloured cottages and drystone walls, but I was utterly beguiled by the beauty of what it represented. After the upheaval of the previous decade, these 90 metres of mortgaged bricks and mortar were a symbol of stability; a safe haven for me and my boys.

It's not as if we were ever without a home, but when their father and I divorced, I was the one who left. In retrospect, I know it was the right decision. The house we had bought together in fulfilment of the 'let's move to the country so the kids can run free and we can raise chickens' dream was a project. By which I mean a wreck, damp of wall, crumbling of rafter and leaking of roof. Together, we were equal to the challenge – husband number one is a fantastically competent amateur builder and I was there to keep the kids out of the way. Apart, only one of us was capable of stopping the place from falling down.

But when life got in the way of the dream, my first instinct was to stay put. This was the children's home and I was their mother. Home and mothering were one and the same. The albeit mouldy walls they had known since they were in infant school were,

I believed, a physical manifestation of my ability to keep them safe. Leaving was a sign that I had failed. Leaving meant that I was not only a bad wife, but a Bad Mother too.

In the end, I found a sweet cottage to rent further up the hill, close enough for the boys to walk between their two homes but far enough away to mean that their dad and I used different routes into and out of the village. It was unfurnished and the landlord was relaxed about me hanging things on the walls, so we were surrounded by our own possessions. I was eager to move in. After a year sharing a house with a man I was divorcing, I relished the idea of my own front door and the boys were thrilled to have a garden level enough to accommodate a trampoline.

The upside of renting is that there is no DIY. I didn't much like the tiles in the kitchen and the bathroom needed an overhaul, but since it wasn't my house, I couldn't change anything and I stopped noticing. Rather than spend my weekends gardening, I could simply enjoy reading the papers on the weedy grass. Nor did I have to worry when the oven blew up and the boiler broke down. Having been a slave to a house project for so long, I found that liberating.

The downside is the insecurity. I had a tenancy agreement, but in the back of my mind there was always the worry that my landlord would want his house back. Divorced and renting felt like a vulnerable place to be.

As well as writing about hygge as a social phenomenon, Jeppe Trolle Linnet has also explored how the atmosphere of the concept is created. In his article 'Cozy Interiority; The Interplay of Materiality and Sociality in the Constitution of Third Place Atmosphere', he explains that the term 'hygge' is more often used to describe people's experience of a place than the actual physical appearance of the place itself.[7] Yes, a hyggelig home should be cosy and pleasing to the eye but, first and foremost, it should be an oasis; a place which makes its inhabitants feel protected from the outside world. My ever-present concern about my landlord's return meant that I did not feel protected by my rented cottage, which meant that pretty little house with its sunny kitchen was not, in fact, an entirely hyggelig place to be. I didn't know it at the time, but I did know that it didn't feel quite like home.

The bungalow, on the other hand, does tick the hyggelig box, and it has felt like home from the moment I collected the keys. Even when it was empty and still wore its hint-of-turquoise walls. Even with the mosaic tiles that made the bathroom so cold you could hardly bear to take your clothes off. Even when I discovered that the roof space was full of rats – although I have to confess that the idea of selling up did cross my mind as I lay in bed listening to them above my head, too terrified to sleep lest they chew their way through the ceiling and land on my duvet. (I have since realised that another reason I felt so instantly at home here is that it reminds me of the first house I ever lived in: a 1960s flat-roofed end-of-terrace with an open-plan kitchen-diner and open-tread staircase where I would sit, legs dangling, and play offices. I don't have any stairs here but the architectural echoes are strong and comforting.)

The sense that I had failed in my duty to provide my boys with a safe haven left me the day we moved in. The fact that, at the time, the boys were almost fledged is beside the point; I had been needing to make us a nest for the past eight years and now I could. They went about their busy lives from this base just as they had from the previous one. They appreciated the deck on the rare days when the weather allowed for a bit of an indoor-outdoor merger, but they seemed no more cocooned here than they had in the rented cottage.

I, on the other hand, felt so cocooned in my oasis that for the first twelve months I could barely bring myself to leave.

∧∨∧

Enough of the symbolism. Hygge does indeed describe the abstract notion of home more articulately than anything else I have come across, but it also sums up the idea of home through the distinctly un-abstract medium of interior decoration. As Jonathan Yorke Bean, Assistant Professor of Markets, Innovation and Design at Bucknell University observes in his PhD paper 'Consuming Hygge at Home': 'Hygge has a strong relationship to the material arrangement and use of the home. Hygge influences everything from the size and shape of the dining table to the relationship of the living room to the front door.'[8]

I asked lots of Danish people to tell me what they thought constituted a hyggelig interior. Every one of them began by talking about the weather. The British talk about the weather too, of course, but where for us it is merely an inconvenience – too wet, too dry, too warm for Christmas, too cold for August – the Danes experience the weather in a way that informs both their behaviour and their aesthetics. The long winters mean that their homes are designed with shelter in mind. A hyggelig home must have at least one cosy nook furnished with a squashy sofa and plenty of throws to act as a buffer against the rain and the snow. Danish furniture tends to be made from warm, natural materials and its forms are often rounded, womb-like and embracing.

The inclement weather also dictates that they spend a lot of time snuggled up inside these homes. 'The climate means that we have developed an inside culture,' explains Knud Erik Hansen, Chief Executive Officer of furniture brand Carl Hansen & Søn, 'one that revolves around the home. We even socialise at home rather than in bars and restaurants.' (There is a somewhat un-hyggelig knock-on effect to that: visitors to Copenhagen on a Sunday evening in February can find themselves forced to buy a picnic of bread and cheese from a supermarket after an hour's fruitless wandering through the sleet-drenched streets in search of a welcoming restaurant. Or any restaurant at all. Bread and cheese eaten in a warm bed with a view of the Black Diamond Library on the other side of the water does have a certain hyggelig charm, but we were hoping not to have to improvise. We were looking for open fires, candles and convivial company; we were in the home of hygge, after all.)

After the weather, my interview sample talked about light – a related obsession given the fact that for several months each year the sun doesn't rise until 9 a.m. and has set again by mid-afternoon. Hyggelig light is soft and warm, imitating the tone and colour of the natural summer light that is in such short supply – as the anthropologist Judith Friedman Hansen comments in her book about cultural practices in Denmark, for hygge to exist, 'illumination should be neither too bright nor too dark'.[9]

Modernist lighting designer Poul Henningsen's creations, which are still made by Louis Poulsen, are commonplace in Denmark, as I discovered. Sculptural yet understated, these lights are certainly beautiful objects, but the reason they are still in such widespread use is because they diffuse the light in a totally hyggelig way. Henningsen began his career just as electric light was arriving in Danish homes, and he became fascinated by the impact that this new, artificial light could have on people's sense of well-being.

He believed that electric bulbs were too harsh for private homes, so he came up with the idea of layered shades that would spread the light altogether more softly and naturally.

The quality of the light is crucial, but the way it is used can affect the existence – or not – of hygge, too. Hyggelige spaces are cosy and intimate, and lights are often positioned so that they create a boundary around a specific area. It's common in Danish cafés, for example, to find pendant lamps hanging low over the tables, each pool of light creating a separate, enveloping enclosure.

Natural materials are another hygge essential. The modern masters crafted their furniture from wood – mostly teak, which was in plentiful supply after the war thanks to the cargoes arriving on warships returning from Asia – and it is a tradition that has continued in contemporary Danish design. Rich woods speak of warmth like little else, and besides, as Carl Hansen & Søn's Knud Erik Hansen says, 'when we spend all day surrounded by artificial materials, we want our homes to offer something more natural, so we seek out wood, leather and wool.' Hansen also cites the symbolic warmth that using nature's own materials brings. After all, nothing warms our cockles quite like the feeling that we're doing our bit for the planet.

Apart from a handcrafted object, that is. Few people can fail to have noticed that craft is having a moment in the spotlight. From furniture and home accessories to shoes and cars via crisps, coffee and beer, there is nothing that can't now be made more desirable by the addition of the word 'craft'. It's a reaction to the digital age and the homogeneous retail landscape; a recognition that the convenience of online shopping and the reassuring knowledge that our Starbucks Flat White will taste the same wherever we are in the world have a downside. We feel that we are losing touch with human touch, so we look for products that bear the mark of their makers. Or at least the signature of some canny hipster entrepreneur.

Handmade products speak of authenticity and quality. Doing it yourself is the ultimate in hygge; the process of throwing your own pot or sewing your own quilt fulfils the requirement for mental presence (a topic I will come to later), and the finished piece not only carries your personal mark, it is also imbued with the memories of its making. However, buying hand-thrown cereal bowls or hand-sewn quilts direct from their makers comes a close second, since we connect with that person each night as we climb beneath their quilt, or every morning as we fill their bowl with muesli. Such connections are important in the making of a hyggelig home.

∧∨∧

I hadn't come across hygge when I moved into the bungalow, and I didn't even focus particularly on making the place look cosy, although I was very concerned about its ambient temperature. My previous Cotswold homes had been freezing – for period windows and original stone floors read time-expired and not suitable for interiors. I got chilblains on my fingers that first winter in the project/wreck, and took to turning the oven on full whenever I was in the kitchen. Having left, I was determined never to live in a house that required me to scrape ice off the inside of a window again.

I did have a decorative plan. I had never owned a house on my own before, and the freedom to do exactly as I pleased was thrilling. (I consulted my two boys in a pretence at democracy, but fortunately, beyond their own rooms, they were easy about floor colours and furniture placement.) I wanted a home that made me smile when

I walked in and that expressed my bipolar taste – I am equal parts pattern-loving maximalist and Le Corbusian minimalist. The tiny hallway is wrapped in bronze-tinted wallpaper featuring climbing roses and caged songbirds. It has a lime-green rubber floor. (Look closely and you will see that the songbirds' feathers are the same citrus hue.) The dark grey walls of my bathroom are covered with formal Victorian portraits in ornate gold picture frames. The open-plan kitchen/eating/living space is a white backdrop for a mismatched selection of inherited vintage, contemporary and inevitable IKEA furniture. And Sid, the driftwood man I bought from his maker, whose articulated arms are made from wood found on my favourite Dorset beach. These arms can be adjusted into a variety of expressive positions; jaunty is my favourite, but hands-on-hips feisty is a good look too. The floors appear to be made from wide walnut boards, but are in fact some kind of easy-clean vinyl, and the passageways between the rooms have wallpapered walls. As does my hexagonal work hut. This hut is small and can be draughty when the wind blows, as it often does since I live on top of a hill, but I have always hankered after a writing room and now I have one. With gloriously patterned walls and a view.

I would like to replace the plastic-framed patio doors with something a bit more contemporary (and that doesn't involve use of the word 'patio'), and I have vague plans to put a shower in the bathroom by the boys' rooms so they don't have to share mine, but essentially I am done with home improvements. I like the way the bungalow looks and I like living in it even more. It is easy to live in. Comfortable; accommodating. In *The Architecture of Happiness* Alain de Botton writes that 'a piece of domestic architecture, no less than a mosque or a chapel, can assist in the commemoration of our true selves'.[10] He is right. I may not have made this home with hygge in mind, but it does feel like a commemoration of my true self, and that seems pretty hyggelig to me.

Once I discovered hygge, I looked at my house again and was interested to see that it has other hyggelige qualities, too. There's the open-plan layout, for a start. Open-plan homes were another brilliant post-war innovation and even the most ordinary homes of the period benefited from this more modern, family-focused way of thinking about housing. To avoid lots of separate rooms which shut people off from each other, architects started building homes with generous, multifunctional open spaces where families could cook, eat and play together. Sociable, egalitarian and practical, open-plan homes are the architectural manifestation of hygge.

At least, they are if the inhabitants have zoned. Those industrial lofts of the 1990s with concrete floors large enough and empty enough to skateboard over are not hyggelig at all. Hygge favours open-plan because it encourages family togetherness, but everything else about hygge centres on the small, the cosy and the intimate. Zoning is a neat solution to this dichotomy; rather than ruin the sociability of family-friendly open-plan rooms by erecting walls, the idea is to use the furniture to create intimate areas within the larger space. Finn Juhl was a huge fan of zoning (although I doubt he used the term), specifically designing his furniture to look good from all angles so that it could be arranged in a friendly cluster in the centre of the room and not around the edge like lines of lonely teenagers at a 1980s school disco.

Some Danes take this zoning thing even further. In *We are a Little Land*, Judith Friedman Hansen describes how a woman she interviewed made herself a 'hyggekrog' (a hygge nook) whenever her sailor husband was away on a trip. Just as small children build themselves camps using tablecloths and blankets, this woman made herself a private den by hanging curtains around a small corner of her living space. I am more of roller blind person myself (and claustrophobic to boot), so I wasn't sure about a hyggekrog, but I did decide to try a bit of zoning using an IKEA Billy bookcase tipped on its side. This has created a mini wall between the 'talking round the fire' and the 'slobbing in front of the TV' bits of my kitchen-dining-sitting room, and it has made a difference; the TV zone is a very cosy place to hang out.

I don't have any Danish furniture, but I do have a lot of simple, functional wooden pieces and the 'talking round the fire' area is lit by a layered lampshade that diffuses the light in a way that would, I believe, have met with Poul Henningsen's approval. I don't really do candles as I find the flickering light gives me a migraine, but I do use the wood-burning stove on winter evenings and, on particularly miserable days, I have even been known to abandon the hut in favour of working by the fireside. I also have a great deal of wobbly handcrafted crockery bought from makers whose names I know, and the window-sills are home to displays of unexceptional objects rich in personal meaning. A beaded snowflake made years ago by my youngest son; a piece of driftwood brought back from the first holiday I had with my boyfriend; the wooden spoon I bought when I left home and which has stirred almost every meal I have cooked since.

But it turns out that probably the most hyggelig thing of all about my bungalow is not the abundance of commemorative clutter, the wooden furniture or even the cosy zones. It is its lack of grandeur.

Jeppe Trolle Linnet's intriguing paper on hygge contains a short section entitled 'Small Means Facilitate Hygge'. 'Several Danish authors have remarked how the hygge mood is a "fickle guest",' he writes, 'that leaves if things become too high-strung, manipulated, or status-orientated . . . Thus, while in Danish society many people currently live lives characterised by material abundance and high levels of private consumption, the cultural values of simplicity and "making-do" show continuity to this day . . . Hygge is antithetical to excess. There may be no showing off in relation to hygge.'[11]

You could argue that seeking to be simpler than the Joneses is just a different way of showing off. (Linnet flags up a rather sanctimonious tendency among the hygge-channelling middle classes to look down on those who flash the cash because they regard them as having lost the essence of real hyggelig togetherness.) However, it is certainly true that an overly grand, wealth-asserting house is often an uncomfortable one to be in. Those too-perfect places with rules about shoes and bathroom taps you can't turn on – or off. Bright white, out-of-a-magazine houses that make you nervous about sitting down.

I stayed in one once. I was writing a piece about it for one of the colour supplements, and since it was in the South of France, I had to stay over. (I know, tough job.) It was extraordinarily beautiful with vast, glossy white rooms opening seamlessly on to glossy white terraces. The many sofas and floor cushions and sun loungers and hammocks suggested a life of endless, sun-soaked leisure. All I could think of was what would happen if I spilled my espresso. Which, being so tense, I did.

To be hyggelig, a home must wear its beauty quietly. It must be a comfortable and comforting backdrop to life, and on no account must it frighten anyone into upsetting their coffee. I am not averse to a little unnecessary glamour, and I do have a wish list of statement furniture in my head in case of an unexpected windfall, but one of the things I like most about the bungalow is its lack of pretension.

Some people would call it ugly, including no doubt that floral-valance-loving Polish woman in her bed and breakfast in Wales, but I disagree. A rectangular box with a mossy roof and plastic windows, the place certainly isn't beautiful, but since it has no architectural ambition beyond its functions of providing shelter, warmth and a remarkable view – functions it fulfils – it can't offend. It isn't Danish in any immediately recognisable sense, but its modest utility does, I believe, have echoes of Finn Juhl.

Having decided to try to live a more hyggelig life, I was naturally delighted to discover that my house was already on the right track. But as I curled, self-satisfied, into the comfortable depths of my round-sided chair, I realised that that was the point. There isn't anything particularly special about hygge's approach to homemaking; the desire to live somewhere warm and comfortable, somewhere that we find aesthetically pleasing and that speaks of who we are is age-old and universal – all hygge does is give that desire a set of tenets and a name. Hygge is far too self-effacing a concept to impose itself on anyone, but by expressing the notion of home so clearly, it does encourage people to pay attention to just what it is that makes a house a home.

'*Hygge occurs when you are alone, enjoying a cup of coffee or reading a good book, as well as when you are having a good time with people you like. This morning my study group and I gathered to work on our project. One of the girls spontaneously brought home-made bread and I brought tea and coffee. Suddenly the framework for today's group was completely changed – and I found the situation very hyggelig*'

# HOW TO HYGGE:
## BY DESIGN

# DANISH MODERN – THE NAMES TO KNOW

'In the 1940s most people in Denmark still connected the concept of hygge with a home full of large upholstered furniture and curtains,' Thomas Graversen, Owner and Chief Creative Officer of the furniture brand Fredericia told me when we spoke about hygge's place in the Danish Modern movement. 'So when Børge Mogensen and his peers set out to rationalise the homes of the Danes, many people thought that they would lose hygge.'

As it turned out, nothing could have been further from the truth. Danish Modern, with its simple lines, human focus and quiet beauty has come to embody Denmark's design aesthetic, both at home and abroad, and is therefore the interior style most commonly associated with the idea of hygge.

Denmark's people understand, love and live with their design heritage, so if you want your home to whisper hygge like a Dane's, these are the key names and the important pieces of furniture that you need to know. (There is a Where to Buy directory on pages 219–21.)

## Kaare Klint, 1888–1954

Architect and designer Kaare Klint is considered to be the father of Danish Modern. He was instrumental in founding the furniture school at the Royal Academy of Fine Arts in Copenhagen in 1924 where subsequently, as Professor of Architecture, he helped to shape many of the great names of Danish Modern's golden age, including Poul Kjærholm and Børge Mogensen.

Klint's design philosophy was rooted in tradition and focused on the future. Modern furniture, he advocated, came out of close analyses of the human form, its proportions and requirements, coupled with a thorough understanding of the craftsmanship of the past. (He would frequently take his students to see the historical furniture collection at the Danish Museum of Art and Design, now Designmuseum Danmark). His approach put him at odds with the Bauhaus designers, who sought to cut themselves off from design history in order to create a whole new aesthetic, but it set the path for Danish Modern. Klint's designs are characterised by a harmonious balance between form and materials and also by their relationship to their environment; quietly beautiful, his pieces never dominate the room in which they are placed.

### What to look out for

The Faaborg Chair: one of his earliest and most famous pieces, the Faaborg Chair was originally designed in 1914 and is still produced by Rud. Rasmussen today. This oak and woven cane chair was one of the first pieces of Danish furniture to strip away unnecessary decoration and focus solely on form and function.

The Safari Chair: Klint was inspired by the simple utility of traditional folding safari chairs, and his version (one of the world's first self-assembly chairs) loses none of that functional charm. Designed in 1933, it is produced today by Carl Hansen.

LK 101 Pendant Light: Klint was a craftsman and his furniture was handmade using traditional cabinetmaking techniques. However, he was also interested in designing for mass production and in the 1940s, helped by his son Ebsen, he created a series of technically challenging folding paper lampshades for the firm Le Klint. The LK 101 is now one of the company's bestselling designs.

*Faaborg Chair*

# Poul Henningsen, 1894–1967

Poul Henningsen began his professional life in architecture, but by the 1920s his interests had turned to lighting and the role it played in people's sense of well-being. Electricity had just started to arrive in Danish households and, while the early lights provided a solution to the problem of how to see after dark, the quality of the light they cast was harsh and unpleasant. PH, as he was known, was determined to improve things and devoted his life to studying how he could bring comfort and ambience to the electrified light bulb.

His theory was that light should be as close to natural daylight as possible, and that people should not be subjected to a bulb's direct glare. Working with the lighting manufacturer Louis Poulsen (who still produce his designs today), he began to make lights with layered shades. These groundbreaking shades not only concealed the bulb, they also diffused the light and brought a touch of sculptural elegance to the rooms they illuminated.

*What to look out for*

PH Artichoke Light: designed in 1958 for the Langelinie Pavillion restaurant in Copenhagen (where they still hang today), the PH Artichoke consists of 72 precisely positioned metal leaves arranged in 12 unique rows and provides 100 per cent glare-free light. It is also rather beautiful.

PH 5: Designed on the principle of a reflective three-shade system, which directs the majority of the light downwards, the PH 5 pendant is intended to hang low over dining tables. The Classic version features a red cone and small blue reflector to create a pleasingly warm tone of light. First designed in 1958, it is still a bestseller.

*PH Artichoke Light*

*PH 5 Light, designed by Poul Henningsen*

## Børge Mogensen, 1914–72

Initially trained as a cabinetmaker, Børge Mogensen studied at the Royal Academy of Fine Arts under Kaare Klint, graduating with a degree in architecture in 1942. He established his own studio in 1950 and, shortly afterwards, began to collaborate with the interior architect Andreas Graversen. By 1955, Graversen had acquired the furniture producers Fredericia and from that point on, Mogensen designed chiefly for Fredericia's workshop.

Heavily influenced by Klint's functional, craft-centred approach, Mogensen's aesthetic was simple and clean. He used natural materials such as oak and leather and applied cabinetmaker's details to industrially produced furniture. His driving ambition was to create everyday furniture that would enrich people's lives and endure for generations. Fredericia still produces many of Mogensen's designs today.

*What to look out for*

The Spanish Chair: Mogensen designed this sturdy wood and saddle-leather chair in 1958, inspired by a traditional chair he had seen time and again while travelling through Spain. His idea was to dispense with the clutter of side and coffee tables by designing armrests broad enough to accommodate a glass or book.

J39: Otherwise known as 'The People's Chair' because of its universal appeal, this wooden chair, with its handwoven paper cord seat, is Mogensen's most successful design and perhaps the best-known chair in Denmark. It was first designed in 1947 and has been in continuous production ever since.

2213 Sofa: determined to create the ultimate sofa, Mogensen initially designed the prototype for this sofa for his own home. He was so pleased with the result that he sent it to Fredericia for production and it has been part of the company's collection since 1962.

## Hans Wegner, 1914–2007

A contender for the title of Denmark's best-known designer, Hans Wegner had craft in his bones. He was the son of a shoemaker, and began his professional training as an apprentice to a cabinetmaker in Jutland. Like many of the Danish greats he too studied architecture, spending three years at Copenhagen's Architectural Academy before joining Arne Jacobsen and Erik Møller (two more luminaries of the period) making furniture for the distinctly Modernist town hall in Aarhus.

In 1940 he began working with the master craftsman Johannes Hansen. It was Hansen who put the first of Wegner's chairs into production and set the course for his subsequent career. In the years following the Second World War, Wegner designed some five hundred chairs, all expressing the very essence of Danish Modern – a combination of highly functional modernity combined with exquisite craftsmanship rooted in tradition. Wegner worked on the principle that a chair should be a work of art made to support the human form.

*What to look out for*

The Wishbone Chair: Wegner's most successful design, the Wishbone Chair, is part of a series inspired by Chinese chairs from the Ming dynasty. With its characteristic Y-shaped back and simple paper cord seat, it is light, comfortable, modern – and deceptively difficult to make. (Hand-weaving 120 metres of paper cord is just one of the 100 different stages involved.) The Wishbone has been in continuous production at Carl Hansen & Søn since 1950.

The Shell Chair: first designed in 1963, the Shell Chair divided opinion; design critics loved its wing-like lines and arching, tapered legs, but consumers found it too avant-garde for their homes and sales were

*Wishbone Chair*

slow. However, when it was reissued in 1998, it was an immediate hit thanks to its combination of lightness, stability and comfort.

The CH29 Chair: popularly known as the 'Sawbuck Chair' because its legs resemble those on the sawbucks (or sawhorses) traditionally used by carpenters and woodcutters, CH29 was originally designed in 1952. Like so many of Wegner's pieces, it is a combination of simplicity, comfort and a unique aesthetic.

*CH29 Chair*

*Shell Chair*

## Arne Jacobsen, 1902–71

The architect and designer Arne Jacobsen is probably the most modern of all the Danish Modernists. His designs were without doubt beautifully made, but they built on his country's new design heritage rather than the cabinetmaking traditions of the past.

An architect by training, Jacobsen was an admirer of Modernists such as Le Corbusier and Mies van der Rohe, and their functionalist approach can be seen in his first major architectural project, the Bella Vista housing scheme in Copenhagen, completed in 1934. But Jacobsen was also interested in the objects that furnished his buildings and, from the 1950s onward, started designing furniture and objects which made the most of newly emerging techniques such as moulding. Charles Eames was exploring similar territory in the US, but Jacobsen brought a soft and modest elegance to moulded plywood and fibreglass that was noticeably Danish in its sensibility.

### What to look out for

The Ant Chair: launched in 1952, the Ant's distinctive, insect-like form came about because Jacobsen wanted to break new ground by making the back and seat of his chair from a single piece of steam-bent plywood. The manufacturers, Fritz Hansen, obliged and furniture history was made.

The Swan Chair: designed in 1958 for the lobby and lounge areas of his glass-encased SAS Hotel in Copenhagen (Jacobsen designed every element of the hotel, both inside and out), the Swan Chair has no straight lines at all.

The Egg Chair: a sister to the Swan, the Egg's cocooning form is due to its moulded fibreglass shell. Its soft, womb-like shape was the perfect antidote to the hard, straight lines of the SAS Hotel (now the Radisson Blu Royal Hotel Copenhagen) it was designed to furnish.

## Finn Juhl, 1912–89

The first Danish furniture designer to achieve international recognition, Finn Juhl was self-taught as a designer (he studied architecture at the Royal Academy of Fine Arts in Copenhagen) and began by making furniture for his personal use. However, after setting up his own office in 1945, he soon acquired a reputation as a maker of expressive and sculptural pieces clearly influenced by modern abstract art.

Working mostly in teak, he shared the Danish Modernists' view that furniture had above all to be comfortable. 'It is fundamental that furniture is practical,' he said.

*Chieftain's Chair*

### What to look out for

The Chieftain's Chair: designed in 1949, this is probably Finn Juhl's best-known piece. The sculpturally shaped seat and back are separate from the wooden frame, a characteristic shared by many of Juhl's chairs.

Silver Table: Juhl designed this walnut table in 1948 for his own home, but it was put into production in the late 1950s. Its oval shape makes it perfect for non-hierarchical entertaining.

*Finn Juhl's Silver Table*

## Poul Kjærholm, 1929–80

Poul Kjærholm trained at the Danish School of Arts and Crafts in Copenhagen, but he called himself a 'furniture architect' rather than a designer because, like Arne Jacobsen and Finn Juhl, he believed that buildings were formed both by their structure and the things inside them. 'Furniture should intervene as a defining factor in existing spaces and transform them into Places,' he said; 'rooms that people can occupy; rooms where human relations can be clarified and rendered visible.'

Kjærholm was particularly interested in industrial materials, especially steel, which he regarded as a natural material with the same artistic fineness as wood. Although he turned his back on the craft tradition, designing exclusively for mass production, the exquisite detail of his work gives the impression that it has been made by hand.

*What to look out for*

PK22 Lounge Chair: the combination of steel frame and leather upholstery is typical of Kjærholm – as is the piece's discreet and elegant aesthetic. Immediately successful (it was awarded the 1957 Grand Prix at the Milan Triennale, the world's premier design fair), the PK22 is the chair that launched his career.

PK80 Daybed: one of Kjærholm's most sophisticated and iconic designs, the PK80 Daybed is striking in its utter simplicity; devoid of almost all detailing, it is about the perfect balance of construction and materials. In 2004, the Museum of Modern Art in New York bought one for their galleries, thus acknowledging the daybed's natural place in furniture history.

## Nanna Ditzel, 1923–2005

As Danish Modern's only woman, Nanna Ditzel stood out from the start. Having trained first as an apprentice cabinetmaker in Copenhagen and then at the city's Royal Academy of Fine Arts, she had all the right credentials, and she combined her technical skill and historical knowledge with an insightful eye for the mode of production.

Ditzel was always experimental. She embraced new materials and technologies that were emerging in the 1950s and 1960s to create furniture that looked as good as it felt to use. 'It is very important to take into account the way a chair's appearance combines with the person who sits in it,' she said. 'Some chairs look like crutches. And I don't like them at all.'

*What to look out for*

Children's Toadstool: rounded forms were Nanna Ditzel's signature. Designed in 1962, this stackable little stool was the result of her observation that 'children never sit still for two minutes. They get up, stand on the chair and subsequently it tips over.' It has a fond place in many Danish homes and is now produced by Snedkergaarden.[12]

Hanging Egg Chair: Nanna Ditzel broke new ground when she designed this ovoid wicker chair; never before had wickerwork been moulded into so round a form. Launched in 1959, it is produced today by Sika Design.

*Nanna Ditzel's Hanging Chair™*

The Danish Modern tradition continues to flourish today. Many of the original designs from the 1940s, 1950s and 1960s are still in production, updated to fit modern standards where necessary (several of Poul Henningsen's lights now come with LEDs, for example), and there is also a whole new generation of designers who are taking the legacy forward into the future. Here are some of the best.

## Carl Hansen & Søn

Founded in 1908 in Odense, Carl Hansen's aim was to provide Danish consumers with well-made, affordably priced modern furniture by combining the country's outstanding craft skills with rational serial production. The idea proved successful and today Carl Hansen & Søn is an international brand. Most of the furniture the company produces was first designed in the golden age of Danish Modern by the likes of Kaare Klint and Hans Wegner. Now made by craftsmen at the factory in Aarup, these pieces have lost none of their appeal.

## Design by Dane

With a cabinetmaker as its creative director, Design by Dane is made in the Danish Modern mould. 'They [the first Danish Modern designers] decided how Danish design should be, and today we are following their rules,' says the company's Art and Design Director Cecilie Brock Johnsen. But while Design by Dane's products are inspired by furniture from earlier generations and made using traditional techniques (there are no screws or seams holding things together; just wood on wood), they are designed for modern life. 'Functionality is a very important factor for the outcome of our designs,' Brock Johnsen explains.

'We make a great effort to design our furniture so it suits the human body and satisfies the needs we have. For example, the next piece in our collection is a stool that can be hung on the wall. A lot of people live in small apartments, so this will be both a wall piece and an extra chair.'

## dk3

Established in 2009, DK3 combines new work with reissues of furniture by some of Danish Modern's greatest names, including Kaare Klint and Børge Mogensen. 'I love the idea of having the classics and mixing them with new designs,' says the company's founder and designer Jacob Plejdrup. 'I am lucky to carry that magnificent legacy as part of my portfolio, but I don't draw a line between the two; the new pieces are continuing the tradition because they are shaped by nature and crafted by true enthusiasts.'

## Fredericia

Fredericia first started in 1911, but the company people know today launched in 1955 when the current owner's father, Andreas Graversen, took over and began a long-standing collaboration with the designer Børge Mogensen. Fredericia still produces many of his pieces today, along with new furniture by a broad range of international and Danish designers. 'We are proud to continue the legacy of Mogensen,' says owner and Chief Creative Officer Thomas Graversen, 'not only by reproducing his designs and keeping them up to date with current trends and standards, but also by adapting his principles to the new products that we develop.'

## Fritz Hansen

Fritz Hansen can trace its history back to 1872 when the eponymous founder, a cabinetmaker, obtained a licence to trade in Copenhagen. In the first fifty years, his company made furniture for many of Denmark's most prestigious buildings, including the University Library in Copenhagen.

Fritz Hansen was a key player in Danish Modern, working with Hans Wegner, Arne Jacobsen and, in the 1960s, Piet Hein, creator of perhaps the most democratic of dining tables, the curvaceous Superellipse. The company still produces all of these classics, and also works with a roster of contemporary designers who create modern pieces filled with the company's traditional spirit under the label Republic of Fritz Hansen.

## HAY

Launched in 2002, HAY is now a global corporation employing hundreds of people, but it has not lost sight of its founding aim, which is to provide meaningful products made from quality materials and designed with a joyful aesthetic. As you would expect from a design company set up in Denmark, HAY's furniture is rooted in tradition and craftsmanship, but it also seeks to push boundaries. As the website says: 'HAY looks back with pride at the age of Danish Modern where quality, craftsmanship and humanistic design put Denmark on the global map, and we look with excitement to the future as we explore the current possibilities of new technologies, new materials and new ways of living.'

## Louis Poulsen

Louis Poulsen had existed as a company for several years before lighting designer Poul Henningsen joined in 1925, but his arrival was the moment that shaped its future. Henningsen's first light, the PH Luminaire (made in collaboration with Louis Poulsen), won a gold medal at the International Exhibition for Decorative Arts in Paris. Designed to provide a warm light that was as close to natural daylight as possible, the Luminaire was an expression of a new lighting philosophy that went on to secure Louis Poulsen's reputation both at home and abroad.

Today the company mixes classics with new lighting solutions by a wide range of international designers. Poul Henningsen's philosophy, which is summed up by the key words function, comfort and ambience, can be seen in every piece. 'PH initiated what later developed into our lighting philosophy back in the late 1920s,' says Brand Manager David Obel Rosenkvist. 'We are proud of this, and the essence of our work is still to make comfortable lighting which makes people beautiful and creates an excellent atmosphere. Human-friendly lighting, in other words.'

*PH Artichoke Light, Poul Henningsen*

# HYGGE BY DESIGN: THE KEY PRINCIPLES

## 1  Warm light

'Cosy, warm light is essential to a hyggelig home,' says designer and spacemaker Tine Mouritsen, 'so the most important thing is that there is light in every corner.' This calls for a mix of pendant, table and floor lamps that will produce layers of ambient light.

In an ideal world, hygge seekers would light their homes with a selection of Poul Henningsen's multi-shade designs – perhaps the PH Artichoke with its distinctive leaves on the ceiling; a mouth-blown white glass PH 2/1 table lamp or two and a PH 80 standing tall in a dark corner, its red-hued reflector giving the light an even warmer glow. But the world is not ideal, so for those of us who cannot illuminate our homes with Danish design classics, the two key things to look for in a light are:

*. . . a diffusing shade*

There are three choices here:

**Henningsen-style layers**  This is a look that has, fortunately, been imitated by numerous designers. If you don't mind a bit of self-assembly, then the Norm 69 by Normann Copenhagen is a modestly priced homage to Henningsen's Artichoke rendered in non-flammable plastic.

**A soft-backed shade**  Rigid lining materials tend to be opaque, which means the light is bounced around the inside of the shade and forced up through the top and bottom. Paper or fabric lining, on the other hand, allows light to pass through the shade itself, creating a much softer effect.

**A light diffuser**  Cheap and readily available, these handy discs are designed to be popped into the bottom ring of a pendant shade, covering the bulb and instantly turning harsh glare into hyggelig glow.

### . . . a warm bulb

Most bulbs emit 'white' light, but the temperature of that light can vary from warm to cool. Incandescent bulbs use heat to generate light and therefore naturally produce a warmer glow, while other technologies such as LED can accommodate multiple-colour temperatures. Colour temperature is measured in degrees kelvin (the lower the value, the warmer the colour) and is denoted by a numerical figure followed by the letter 'k': 2,700k, which is similar to the standard incandescent bulb, will give you cosy.

But you cannot hygge by electric light alone. Heating is marvellous, of course, but radiators and warm floors don't draw us in quite the same way as a flickering flame, which is why we have gathered around fires for comfort ever since we first learned how to make a spark.

An open fire or wood-burning stove will give any room a cosy focal point, so if you have one, use it, and if not, consider having one installed. (Top tip for the chimney-less and anyone who doesn't want the bother of wood and ash – fake fires are fab.)

And don't forget the candles. Mass them in the fireplace, create clusters on the table and scatter tea lights across every available surface. The Danes burn candles all the time, not just on special occasions, so if you want a shortcut to hygge chic, you need to follow their lead.

## 2 Cosy zones

When it comes to the layout of your home, you need to think small. Hygge may mean a great deal more than cosy, but cosy is definitely a big part of it, and you can't do cosy in a cavernous space. The aim is to create areas that suggest comfort and relaxed sociability.

If you have a small, single-function sitting room then making it hyggelig is pretty straightforward; simply pull the furniture in slightly from the walls, put a rug in the centre of the circle and add some strategically placed ambient lighting around the edges. (A low-slung pendant in one corner and a floor-standing uplight in the other would be a good look.) Finish off with a floor cushion, if there's room, and some soft throws over the backs of the chairs.

In an open-plan or multifunctional room, you will have to work harder – although open-plan is rather hyggelig in itself because it's more sociable to have all the family sharing a single space. The secret of success is zoning, which means using the furniture to create intimate spaces that invite conversation. A fireplace makes an obvious focal point, but you can zone in any corner. Mark out the space with a rug, then add a huddle of chairs placed close enough together so that people can talk to each other without shouting. A couple of big, squashy cushions on the floor will add a sense of comfort and provide additional seating.

And don't stop at the living area. This is your home, a place of intimacy; try a couple of chairs or a two-seater sofa in a corner of the bedroom and a comfy armchair near the bath.

### 3 Modestly beautiful, comfortable furniture

Hyggelig furniture is all about comfort, quality and understated beauty. If you can afford to buy anything mentioned in the previous pages, do, because the Danish mid-century masters were pitch-perfect – as are the contemporary designers who have followed in their wake. (Vintage pieces are hard to find these days, but contemporary editions are readily available – see page 219–21.)

You can still get the hygge look even if your budget won't stretch to a Jacobsen Egg chair. Just make sure that whatever you buy ticks the following boxes:

**Wood.** The richer in tone the better.

**Functionality.** Your furniture must perform – and be seen to perform – the task it was made for. Chairs should be comfortable to sit in and, ideally, rounded of form; tables must be robust enough to withstand years of family meals. Avoid furniture that blurs the boundary between function and art; it may be on-trend, but it is too showy for hygge.

**Simplicity.** This is a look that calls for clean lines and simple forms. Extraneous ornamentation is out.

**Craftsmanship.** The Danes really care about the quality of their furniture, and craftsmanship is part of their country's design heritage. As Knud Erik Hansen, Chief Executive Officer of furniture brand Carl Hansen & Søn says, 'There is comfort in the knowledge that something has been made well and will last long enough to be passed on to our children.'

The two most important pieces of furniture in a hyggelig home are the sofa and the dining table. Sofa-wise, go for something squashy and spacious enough for the whole family. Pile it high with cushions, blankets and throws.

When it comes to tables, think informal and egalitarian. Piet Hein's 1968 Superellipse is the ultimate hyggelig dining table; not only is it a Danish design classic, but its elliptical shape (which was inspired by the congestion-easing roundabout Hein created in Sergel's Square in Stockholm), also means that there is no 'head', so everyone is equal. Superellipse is still manufactured by Fritz Hansen, but any round or oval table would create the same effect.

If you can't do circular, the other option is narrow (the idea being that narrowness brings everyone closer together). Run a bench rather than chairs along either side in the interests of informality and democracy.

## 4 Comforting accessories

Cosy comfort is the look you are going for, so layer up with masses of textiles. Heap the sofa with piles of cushions, chuck a blanket or two over the side of an armchair and lay a rug across your wooden floor. Focus on natural materials with plenty of texture to add visual warmth.

Hyggelige homes should also be personal, a reflection of who you are, and suffused with a comforting sense of the familiar and the domestic. Here are some ideas:

- Cover a wall with family photographs. Matching frames will give the montage a sense of order.

- Curate collections of personal treasures on coffee tables and mantelpieces, or gather them all together in a cabinet of curiosities.

- Focus on the handmade. Handmade objects are very hyggelige. If you can throw a pot or embroider a cushion then go for it, but remember, this is a look that values quality, so buy in or commission unless you have some real skill. (Anything made by children is exempt, of course.) Handmade tableware is a good place to start – after all, nothing says 'home' quite like a slightly imperfect soup bowl.

- Turn your crockery into a domestic display by arranging it on open shelves or in a glass-fronted cupboard.

- Fill a row of glass storage jars with pasta, pulses, sugar and flour – the kind of comforting dry goods that create the impression of nourishing home cooking. (Hide the microwave in a cupboard.)

*'To me, hygge means being together with my wife, our children, our dogs and our friends at home in our warm living room after a nice dinner, good wine and a cup of freshly brewed coffee. We can talk about anything as long as it has a common interest and everybody can take part. We may listen to a nice piece of soft music and the fire may be lit. We are safe, together, and we have no appointments or deadlines to meet within the next twenty-four hours. It may even be snowing or stormy outside, but as long as it is warm and quiet inside, it is beautifully hyggelig!'*

# HYGGE
# LIVING

# HYGGE AND THE ART OF
# NON-HIERARCHICAL COOKING

Talk to a Danish person about hygge and it won't be long before they mention food. Not a specific food, in most cases; more the use of food as a way of gathering together family and friends. There is nothing more hyggelig, it seems, than sharing a meal with those you love.

I grew up in a family who believed that mealtimes mattered. When we were small, my brother and I would eat supper earlier than our parents, but Mum would sit with us while we ate – Spag Bol, sweetcorn soufflé or, if we were lucky, Findus Crispy Pancakes, the molten cheese filling so hot we scalded our tongues – and we would chat about our day. At the weekends, Saturday lunches and Sunday suppers were family occasions. The four of us would sit around the table together and my stepfather would tell us about wine and how important it was to undercook beef. Saturday nights were dinner party nights. We were not invited, but lying in bed listening to the increasingly raucous laughter, I absorbed the notion that when friends met up, they ate and they drank. As we got older, supper was the time when the four of us came together. Not always harmoniously, but whatever our opposing political, domestic or dietary views, the fact that we sat around the table together on a regular basis meant that we did at least communicate.

I have continued this tradition with my own family. Supper has always been the evening's headline event. It marks the end of the working day, so homework, emails and domestic chores must all be finished with before the food is served. This does mean that sometimes we eat later than is good for us, but the idea that the evening meal is a reward that's not to be rushed is firmly ingrained. I can't pretend that the meals are always culinary extravaganzas – we are overly reliant on pasta, for a start – or that we always have the most erudite of conversations, but the boys and I do sit around the table on a regular basis and, while we're eating, we leave our phones elsewhere.

I am the family cook. This is partly displacement. I am not a fan of housework; I believe that surface tidiness and a jug of fresh flowers on the table can disguise a multitude of housekeeping oversights, so I prove my domesticity by cooking. Some people dust their skirting boards; I bake to create a virtuous circle. An hour spent with the vacuum cleaner and a mop leaves me grumpy and tired and nobody appreciates my efforts until I shout at them to take their bloody shoes off. If I make a cake, everyone is happy.

But I also cook to create visible, smellable, edible signs of home. One of the first things I did when we moved from London to the project/wreck in the country was to make blackberry jam. I set aside an entire afternoon for the practice of this mysterious art. My grandmother had told me that success depended on achieving 'a good set'. She instructed me to put several saucers in the deep freeze and when the time came, I was to spoon some jam onto one of these ice-cold saucers and push it with my finger. She didn't say how I would know the time had come, simply that I should take the jam off the heat as soon as the surface of the test dollop wrinkled. I put ten saucers in the freezer, poured the blackberries and sugar into my specially bought preserving pan and turned on the gas.

Ten minutes later, I removed the first saucer, spooned out some jam, pushed it with my finger and there was the wrinkle. I turned off the gas, poured the jam into the jars and that was that. I felt strangely let down by how easy it had been, but looking at the line of jars cooling on the worktop gave me a deep sense of satisfaction. Our new house was falling down and at the time we were relying solely on my erratic earnings as a part-time freelance writer, but the kitchen was full of home-made jam so all must be well.

As the boys have grown up and become independent, I've used cooking as a way of prolonging motherhood. I am no longer needed to read stories, patch knees or whisper dreams into their ears in the middle of the night, but I can still cook for them. When the eldest comes home, I fill the fridge with his favourite things and send him on his way with home-made supplies. I show my support for them through exams by serving up fish pie (for the omega oil) and baking endless supplies of dark chocolate brownies (for the energy). Conversely, after my first divorce left me childless every other weekend and my second marriage turned me into a stepmother, I found family cooking difficult. I wanted to prove my stepmotherly credentials by turning out a decent roast chicken and apple crumble, but rubbing butter and flour and sugar into sweet crumbs for someone else's boys made me miss my own with an intensity that caused me physical pain.

I love the rituals of cooking, too. They mark the passage of the year, and are a way of rooting us, connecting us with our family history. I am not religious, but I observe Stir up Sunday – the last Sunday before Advent – because it reminds me of my grandmother. She would stand me on a chair in front of the mixing bowl and when all the fruit and the spices and the flour and the sugar were measured out, I would stir, three times clockwise, with a wooden spoon. I must confess that these days I use Dan Lepard's recipe because it features prunes and figs and stout, and sometimes I forget which Sunday is the one before Advent. But there is always a Sunday in late November or early December on which I make the pudding, and when I call the boys to come and stir, I tell them the story of their great-grandmother's famous fruit mix.

All this is deeply hyggelig, but it is also profoundly human. We all use food to create personal and cultural memories, and communal eating has been used to bind social groups together ever since the early hunter-gatherers stopped their wanderings and established the first villages ten thousand years ago. As the developmental psychologist and author Susan Pinker writes in *The Village Effect: Why Face-to-Face Contact Matters*, 'when people share food, they're more likely to feel that they are part of a group and to compromise to resolve a conflict'.[1] However, while hygge may not have a monopoly on these eating rituals, it seems to me that the concept does offer an alternative approach – and it is one that I find rather appealing.

∧∨∧

When I think back to the family Christmases of my childhood, what I remember is the absence of my grandmothers. Their 1970s kitchens were not open-plan, they were working galleys shut away from the rest of the house. My grannies would disappear into these steamy spaces before breakfast, and there they would remain until the feast was done. (We did, occasionally, catch sight of Granny A's head, thanks to a natty serving hatch, which she would peer through from time to time to see how we were all doing.) The drama – the carving of the turkey, the flaming of the pudding – happened at the table and was orchestrated by the men, who sat at its head. When we were done, back the grannies would go, accompanied by the other women and the children, to wash and dry and tidy.

When my mother took over the head chef role she was not stuck in a galley, as we'd gone open-plan by then and it fell to my stepfather to peel the chestnuts, but the main task of making the lunch was still hers and, less naturally domestic than her mother, she found the pressure stressful. Christmas week was a trial, as she worried about how many mince pies to make, whether two stuffings would be enough and how on earth she could co-ordinate things so that both turkey and potatoes would be ready at the same time.

I cooked my first Christmas lunch when I was twenty-nine. I remember nothing of the day – my firstborn's first Christmas – beyond the heat of the kitchen as I strove for festive perfection.

And it wasn't just Christmas. As soon as I became a mother, I felt compelled to mark the high days and holidays of the year with feasts around my table. I gave dinner parties, too. Having friends for supper meant serving them impressive food – towers of this with coulis of that in the 2000s, knowingly old school or flavoured with Sumac and Za'atar in the 2010s – on a pleasingly arranged table covered with ironed Irish linen. They were fun, these gatherings, but trying to be the hostess with the mostest made them awfully hard work and often, by the time my guests arrived, I was exhausted and sick of the sight of the food.

It never occurred to me that there might be another way to do it. A way that did not consign anyone to solitary hours in the kitchen, or involve a week of performance anxiety culminating in a stress-induced headache on the big day itself.

And then I came across hygge. In 'Consuming Hygge at Home', Jonathan Yorke Bean refers to Judith Friedman Hansen's observation that

the typical setting for hygge is a dinner party with close family and friends where guests are drawn close together around a table much narrower than its American counterpart, seated on armless chairs and shared benches close enough that their elbows touch, where alcoholic beverages are poured generously and where food is passed on trays to encourage an atmosphere of conviviality. After dinner, everyone moves to sit around a coffee table, where later on in the evening dessert and coffee will be served.[2]

Hansen, whose dissertation was subsequently published as a book, *We are a Little Land: Cultural Assumptions in Danish Everyday Life*, did her empirical research in the 1970s, but when Bean was in Denmark more recently, he says he found that little had changed.

I like the informality that this description suggests. There's no mention of ironed linen, complicated cutlery arrangements or hierarchical seating plans, and the focus is on conviviality rather than the host's taste in tableware. Passing food around on a tray implies an equally relaxed approach to the meal itself. Hyggelige dinner parties are evidently not about impressing guests with your esoteric taste in seasoning and fancy knife skills. They are about homely food, simply served, and everyone having a good time.

I asked Kell Skött, co-founder of London's only Danish restaurant, Snaps and Rye, what a typical hyggelig menu would look like. He told me that there isn't one – 'hygge is a feeling,' he said. Which may be true, but isn't very helpful for non-Danes such as myself looking for a fail-safe checklist of rules for authentically hyggelig entertaining. My conversations with Danish people have taught me that this illusive hygge feeling is closely linked to a sense of comfort, though, so I think it's reasonable to assume that hygge meals probably feature plentiful platefuls of comfort food.

To be comforting, food should feel good in the mouth and its flavours and aromas should transport the eater back to the place he or she calls home. What these foods will be will vary from individual to individual – in my house, the edible manifestation of home is a tomato sauce made with lots of chilli and fresh thyme and served on pasta bows – but nations also have a shared cuisine; a wealth of eating traditions rooted in the climate and the landscape and which are bound up in their citizens' sense of identity.

Denmark's food culture has been formed by its seven thousand kilometres of coastline and long, cold, dark winters. In the pre-industrial age, there was neither the time nor the appetite for a refined cuisine; both work and climate were physically demanding, so meals had to be hearty and sustaining. Rye was grown in place of wheat, which is less tolerant of low temperatures, and turned into a coarse and highly nutritious black bread known as rugbrød. (It was eaten in hunks with slices of fish before the arrival of bread-slicing machines in the mid-nineteenth century brought about the invention of the now ubiquitous smørrebrød open sandwich.) Salting, smoking and pickling were all commonly used to preserve fish, meat and vegetables to ensure that there was nutritious food for the winter table. (Smoked herring has been made on the Baltic island of Bornholm since the late 1800s, while pickled herring dates back to the Middle Ages.) Potatoes were introduced by the French Huguenots in the early 1800s and became an instant staple.

Today central heating insulates people against the cold and international trade allows us all to eat international ingredients regardless of the season. But while we might have ample opportunity to eat a geographically eclectic diet, when we're seeking comfort we tend to revert to our traditional dishes. In Denmark that means something warm and hearty which is probably either salted or pickled and served with potatoes.

While the food does undoubtedly contribute to the creation of hygge, the atmosphere in which it is made and eaten plays a far bigger role. In his book *The Land of the Living: The Danish Folk High Schools and Denmark's Non-violent Path to Modernization*, Steven Borish writes that 'hygge depends on the complete and positive participation of all present in the encounter'.[3] Borish's observations are more about the importance of mental presence and participation than cooking for Christmas or dinner parties (a point I will explore later), but given the fact that hygge situations so often involve eating with others and, as Hansen observed, the food is usually passed from person to person on these occasions, rather than dished out by a host, I am happy to assume that the requirement for complete participation extends to the preparation of meals and that, therefore, for a food-based event to be truly hyggelig, no single person must be stuck at the stove.

I find that quietly radical. If everyone present has to participate fully, it follows that everyone has to do an equal amount of work. Instead of a few guests doing the host a favour by peeling the potatoes or laying the table, everyone gets properly stuck in. This turns cooking from a chore to be done before the fun begins into a sociable activity in itself. 'Making food together is a special experience which can be categorised as hyggelig,' one of my interviewees told me. 'You might open a bottle of wine and, while you are all working on your dinner together, you talk and joke with each other.'

Group cooking is also wonderfully egalitarian because it does away with the hierarchy of head chef and his or her sous chef and bottle washers. Not only does that take the pressure off a particular person, it also influences the type of food that is made. There may not be any specifically hyggelige foods, but hyggelige meals are generally described as 'homely'. Delicious, yes, and often accompanied by generous quantities of alcohol (as one person I spoke to explained, opening a bottle of wine is a sign that everyone has time to relax), but certainly not fancy. That is largely to do with the role that comfort plays in the creation of hygge, as I've discussed, but it is also because there's no praising of an individual cook in a team effort. And without praise, what's the point of sweating over lamb three ways and a deconstructed lemon tart? You may as well do stew. Or store kolde bord, the buffet-style lunch that is a tradition of family gatherings at Christmas, Easter and Whitsun. The table is laid with buttered slices of rugbrød and a vast selection of toppings, and guests simply assemble their own smørrebrød. Nothing says egalitarian entertaining quite like making your own sandwich.

/\/\/\

I wanted to mark my first Christmas in the bungalow by having the family to me. I had also recently discovered hygge, and thought it would be a good opportunity to put the theory of an egalitarian Christmas to the test. At the start of December, I sent out an email assigning tasks. Mum was to do the smoked salmon and provide the Prosecco. My brother was to bring a ham for the following day (ham for breakfast is a festive family tradition, the origins of which escape me), my half-brother the cheese and my dad and his wife the wine.

My eldest son was in charge of the roast potatoes and the youngest the lemon tart. That left me with the meat, accompanying vegetables and the Christmas pudding. I moved the feast to the day after Boxing Day, cleverly sidestepping the need to cook a turkey, a task I have always found daunting. I'm a vegetarian, and while I am happy to cook meat, I like to do so with as little intervention as possible. Stuffing dead birds and sewing up the hole always feels like too much intervention, so this time I went for Six-hour Lamb in a Bottle of Wine. The recipe is vaguely Middle Eastern, but it has extremely hyggelige qualities: it requires excellent basic ingredients, it is substantial and warming, delicious without being showy and good-tempered if the timing slips, which I discovered is a side effect of cooking as a group.

The run-up was peaceful. I made the Christmas pudding and the mincemeat as usual and when the boys came back we made the mince pies, a mnemonic ritual I instigated when they were small, despite the fact that none of us really likes them. I make and roll the pastry, the eldest cuts the fluted-edged discs and presses them into the baking tray, his brother fills and adds the star-shaped top. When they are cooling on the worktop an hour later, we know that Christmas has begun.

It wasn't hygge all the way, of course. I had a vision of how I wanted the house to look for its first Christmas, but with thirteen coming, plus dog, I realised there was no room for a Danish-style tree blazing with real candles (in the end we went for a small, austere branch wrapped in the simplest of LED fairy lights), and when we were gathered in my quite small house, the crackling fire I had lit to create the ultimate feeling of home made us all so hot that we had to put it out. Which filled the house with smoke.

But we were all together, and even ex-husband number one got involved when we realised that we couldn't cook roast potatoes and Six-hour Lamb in one oven (potatoes want a hot oven, slow-cooked lamb a cool one). Not wanting to ruin the festive season by doing mash, my son took the spuds to his dad's, who delivered them back all crisp and delicious and stayed for a drink for the first time since we divorced.

I have had several hygge-style supper parties since that Christmas. We sit on armless chairs and, if we are more than six, a wooden bench that I keep in the shed. The very narrow table means that our elbows do indeed touch and, since there isn't any room for serving dishes, we have no choice but to pass food from person to person. The set-up is born of necessity rather than a slavish following of the principles of hygge, but it does make for a more informal atmosphere, one that encourages immediate intimacy. I like to invite people who don't know one another, and friendships have been formed over an evening spent eating and drinking cheek-to-cheek.

I don't ask people to bring things, but I have stopped worrying about providing three courses of skill-testing dishes. Since that Six-hour Lamb, I am a one-pot woman. It's curry and stew every time now, followed by a tart made with ready-to-roll pastry, or a plate of cheese and bowls of chocolate. I'm not sure my guests have really noticed the difference, but for me the change has been not life-altering (we're talking supper parties here, after all), but certainly life-enhancing. I have always found sitting around a table laden with good food the best way to socialise and have got pleasure from providing that food, but consciously embracing a more hyggelig attitude has taken out the stress and brought me real joy.

# THERE WILL NEVER BE
# A HYGGE DIET

One of the lovely things about hygge is its liberal attitude towards cake. I am a huge fan of cake, so naturally this endeared me to the concept from the start, but just as I discovered that there is more to hyggelige interiors than candles and blankets, my research has shown me that unashamed cake consumption is simply the icing on a very appealing food philosophy.

According to a post I found on Denmark's official website, Denmark.dk, the Danes eat around ten kilos of cake per person each year. I don't know how that compares with other nations as cake-eating statistics are thin on the ground, but I did read a report in the *Daily Telegraph* which claimed that the Brits bought 110 million cupcakes in 2013;[4] that's roughly two cupcakes per Brit. The average cupcake weighs 87g, apparently, so if the Brits are to match Danish levels of consumption, we each need to consume another 9,000g of non-cupped cake every year. It sounds a lot, but given the nation's expanding waistline I wouldn't be surprised to find that it is a feat we can achieve.

But that's not really the point. The average Dane probably eats about as much cake as the average American, Brit or Swede; what is interesting is that other countries don't advertise their cake consumption on their national websites. The fact that Denmark does indicates that they are proud to be a cake-eating nation.

This is probably because Denmark.dk is a tourist website and, as all tourists know, Denmark is the home of the Danish pastry, or the wienerbrød as it is properly known. (It was first introduced to the country by Viennese bakers in the 1840s when the Danish pastry bakers went on a long-term wage strike, and has since become a national treasure. The pretzel-shaped kringle version is the sign used by Danish bakeries.) But there's something more philosophical behind this, too. Hygge is about taking a break from the pressures and duties of everyday life and, crucially, taking real, unmitigated pleasure in that break, whether it's an hour strolling in the park with a friend or making time for a coffee and a spandauer (a round wienerbrød) in a candlelit café. The idea of a 'guilty pleasure' or 'naughty treat' is anathema to the practice of hygge, and since hygge is ingrained in the Danish psyche, so too, I suggest, is the idea of allowing ourselves regular guilt-free moments of indulgence.

I had a troubled relationship with food throughout my teenage years. Back in the 1980s, calorie-counting was as popular an activity among a certain class of shoulder-padded women as rag-rolling and stippling interior walls and, as an image-obsessed thirteen-year-old desperate to play grown-ups, I naturally followed their lead. It wasn't a happy time. Yes, I could wear skinny jeans, and when I lay on my front I could balance on my hip bones, but standing on the scales twice a day and pretending that a plate of French beans and low-fat yoghurt constituted supper does not make for an easy adolescence. I grew so thin that I delayed the onset of puberty until I was fifteen, and when I started eating again a year later, I discovered that I didn't know when to stop. By the time I was eighteen my hip bones were invisible.

Things settled down once I left school, mostly because I was too busy enjoying student life to think much about food, but the fact that those calorie-fixated years had made me first too thin, then too fat and frightened of food at all times, left me with a deep distrust of diets. Eating is about far more than physical nourishment; it is a multisensory pleasure to be savoured and shared with friends and family. Diets are the precise opposite of all that. Diets are about denial. They strip eating of all its joy and fill the void with guilt.

We are experiencing an obesity crisis here in the UK, so clearly there is something wrong with our eating habits, but I don't believe that diets are the answer. I am neither a psychologist nor a specialist in nutrition, but it seems odd to me that Denmark, despite its citizens' love of pastries and bacon, has one of the OECD's lowest obesity rates (coming in twenty-first out of twenty-nine countries) and almost half that of the UK, for all our faddish food regimes. (In 2012 Denmark's obesity rate stood at 13.1 per cent of the population aged fifteen and over, compared with 26.1 per cent of the UK's, according to OECD Health Statistics 2014.[5])

I am not suggesting that a hyggelig attitude to eating is entirely responsible. The role of poverty in the obesity crisis is well documented – a report by the Fabian Commission on food and poverty, published in March 2015, found that over one fifth of boys and girls from low-income households were classed as obese, compared with 7 per cent for those in the highest income groups.[6] Denmark has the second-lowest poverty rate in the OECD.[7]

The country's high levels of happiness may also play a part, since there is growing evidence to show that there are links between overeating and depression that go both ways. However, there is also a substantial amount of research to suggest that dieting sets up unhealthy relationships with food and that those unhealthy relationships often lead dieters to put on weight, triggering a cycle of failure. (A study by researchers at the University of California, Los Angeles, found evidence that two thirds of people on diets regained more weight than they had lost within four to five years.[8])

The National Centre for Eating Disorders (NCFED) has a report on its website about the emotional effects of dieting.[9] It refers to a study by the American nutrition research pioneer Ancel Keys, the man who first identified the health benefits of a Mediterranean-style diet in the 1950s, into the psychological and physiological effects of drastically reducing food intake. He carried out a series of experiments on healthy young male conscientious objectors (their participation excusing them from military duties during the Korean War) with no history of weight problems. Under the programme, the men ate as normal for three months before having their food intake halved for another three months. They then went through a further three-month rehabilitation period in which they were gradually reintroduced to normal eating. The results of the experiment were far-reaching but, for me, the most interesting findings relate to the men's attitudes to food. During the trial period, all the men involved became obsessed with food and many were driven to guilt-ridden secret eating. When they returned to normal eating habits at the end of the experiment, a high proportion of participants found that they were unable to stop eating even when they were full.

More recent studies have reported similar findings. Peter Herman and Janet Polivy, psychologists at the University of Toronto, to quote one example, tested the willpower of a group of non-dieting students against that of their dieting colleagues. All were invited to eat as much ice cream as they liked, but some were also asked to have one, and in some cases two, milkshakes first. The non-dieters behaved as you would expect, decreasing their ice cream intake in line with the number of milkshakes they had drunk previously. Not so the dieters. Their consumption actually went up, with those having two milkshakes also eating the most ice cream. Herman and Polivy's explanation was that by having the initial milkshake, the dieters felt they had broken their vow of abstinence and so there was little point in refusing the ice cream. Having sinned once, they may as well sin some more.

From a physical point of view, these studies appear to suggest that dieting has an adverse effect on our natural appetite controls. As psychologist Deanne Jade, founder of the NCFED, writes: 'The seeming inability of dieters to stop once they have started stems from the Faustian bargain they made with themselves at the start. Included in the loss of normal internal controls are the normal processes involving satiety. Dieters do not eat interminably once their rules are broken, but they do eat far more than non-dieters do.'[10]

The potential of dieting to upset our inbuilt appetite controls is clearly a problem, but the far bigger issue, as far as I am concerned, is that diets turn food and its consumption into a moral battleground. Just look at the language we use: we are 'good' when we follow the regime; 'bad' or 'naughty' when we slip up. If we don't get thinner, it is a sign that we have 'failed'.

The current fashion for what is termed 'clean eating' takes this to extremes. This approach – which is not about weight loss, apparently, rather a whole new way of looking at food – advocates a diet filled with natural, unprocessed foods. So far, so sensible. However, when some food is classified as 'clean', everything else becomes by definition 'dirty'. Highly processed foods may deserve the label, but I'm not sure about bread, pasta, milk and potatoes. And when apples are considered dirty (too much sugar) then surely things have gone too far.

There is a whole clean eating world on the internet. Its citizens are mostly young women with bouncy hair and glowing skin who live on kale, quinoa, chia seeds, avocado and the occasional bite of raw chocolate. They appear to be in good physical shape, but their lives are dominated by food and its clean credentials: its calorie content, its glycaemic index rating, its lack of trans fat. Taste doesn't seem to come into it, and eating appears to give them no pleasure at all. There isn't anything wrong with what these people eat, but the thinking behind their eating is based on the assumption that food is something to be feared rather than enjoyed. That was exactly how I felt as an adolescent bordering on anorexia, and it wasn't a route to happiness.

The Danes haven't got it completely right. They drink and smoke too much (bars smaller than forty metres square are exempt from the smoking ban and, as I discovered, are very popular and jolly places to spend an evening if you can cope with the fug), factors that at least partly explain why Denmark has one of the lowest life expectancy rates in Western Europe – 82.1 years for women and 78 years for men, according to the World Health Organisation's European Health Report 2015.[11] But the conversations I have had with Danish people indicate that the culture of hygge has at least fostered a healthier attitude to food. It was Meik Wiking, CEO of Copenhagen's Happiness Research Institute, who told me that there would 'never be a hygge diet'.

It is true that hygge is often associated with less healthy foods. A quantitative study into factors affecting the existence of hygge carried out by researcher Heidi Boye for her PhD thesis 'Food and Health in Late Modernity' showed that many people felt that high-sugar, high-fat foods washed down with plenty of alcohol were all key factors in the creation of a hyggelig atmosphere.[12] While that clearly raises issues for Danish dieticians, I believe hygge's embracing attitude towards hedonistic foods brings important mental health benefits. Hygge does not rule that some food is 'dirty', and that the consumption of dirty food must be atoned for with a week of kale smoothies. Feeling guilty about what you eat does not make you thin; it makes you unhappy and obsessive. Hygge replaces guilt with pleasure and fear with enjoyment, and that has to be a good thing.

I got over my eating issues long ago, but what I have spent the last twenty years doing is balancing the calories that go in with the calories I expend in a daily exercise programme. This is a sensible approach for someone who enjoys eating and doesn't want to get fat, but I am a bit obsessive about the calculations. I know how many calories I use on a run, for example, and how many calories there are in a slice of multigrain sourdough bread spread with unsalted butter and apricot jam. If I run before breakfast, I can eat the piece of toast. But if I don't run because there's no time or my back/knee/calf/Achilles is grumbling again, then I get fretful. I know that it will take more than a round of toast on an exercise-free day to make me fat, so I eat, but the aftertaste is guilt-tainted.

When I embarked on my experiment into hygge living, I thought my daily toast and jam habit meant that I had hyggelig eating sorted, but I soon discovered that I was wrong. I realised that my eating was only guilt-free because it was offset by a rigorous exercise routine, and that is not really in the spirit of hygge at all. I am not about to give up running – it is a regular joy that makes me genuinely hungry in a way that reminds me of my childhood, when I would come back from a day on a Cornish beach, sand-covered and scorched by the wind, to devour home-baked rolls and handfuls of peas fresh from the pod. But I have stopped working out how many calories I have burned, and I am making a conscious effort to relax about eating when I have not been for a run. It isn't easy because I see now that so much of the pleasure I get from eating is rooted in the idea of justified reward and, naturally, middle age is taking its toll on my metabolic rate, which I find a bit confronting. But I am making progress. For example, I have discovered that there is pure pleasure to be found from eating Tosca cake (a Nordic speciality – think Bakewell tart without the jam) in the café of Copenhagen's Louisiana Museum, wood-burning stove on one side, view over the Øresund to the coast of Sweden on the other, a few sedentary hours after breakfast. Not every day, but sometimes.

# HYGGE AND THE MYTH OF THE PERFECT FAMILY

Walking through the streets of Copenhagen's Christianshavn district one Monday morning, I was struck by the number of men I saw tricycling their small children to school. (The christiania trike with its roomy, metal-framed cargo box is the preferred mode of family transport for city-living parents in Denmark.) At home, I pass by the village primary school fairly regularly, and a man doing the school run is a rare sight indeed. Rarer still at home time.

Denmark is a famously family friendly society, and its people embraced gender equality long ago. According to the OECD Better Life Index, the female employment rate stands at 78 per cent for women aged 25 to 54, which is among the highest in the OECD countries, while the gender pay gap is one of the lowest.[13] Couples are entitled to 32 weeks of paid parental leave and a place in formal childcare as soon as their baby reaches six months old. There is preschool support from the age of three, and out-of-school care for primary-age children is widely and, crucially, freely available.

Enabling both men and women to pursue careers regardless of their parenting responsibilities is progressive and egalitarian. But it is one thing to set up a system of working-hours childcare and quite another to be truly friendly to families. All too often the reality of both parents working full time is that the kids see more of the nursery or after-school club staff than they do their mum and dad.

Not so in Denmark. After I had got over the surprise of seeing a male-dominated school run, I registered the time. It was 8.45 a.m. These christiania-pedalling dads were not only dropping off their children, they were also working flexitime.

When I got back to the UK I looked into the working habits of the Danes. 'Work–life balance' is a phrase that comes up whenever quality of life issues are raised. The Happiness Research Institute (an independent think tank based in Copenhagen which was set up to explore the causes and effects of human happiness) rates balance as a key indicator. 'The ability to balance working life and family life are crucial for happiness,' it states in its 2014 report 'The Happy Danes'.[14] In the majority of cases, however, the word 'balance' is an imagined ideal rather than an experienced reality. Most people's experience is one of imbalance; the employed have too much of the work and the unemployed too much of the life but no money to enjoy it. In Denmark, the scales are almost level. The Danes enjoy a minimum of five weeks' paid holiday a year and a 37-hour week is not only standard, but widely stuck to – an OECD report published in 2011 revealed that only 2 per cent of Danish employees worked 'very long hours' (defined as over fifty hours per week), compared with an average across OECD countries of 13 per cent.[15] Not only that; flexible working is so routine that it has an official programme, Danish Flexjobs, which is designed to accommodate people who need to work shorter hours. Under the terms of the scheme, employees are paid for effective work done as opposed to hours clocked up. Forget tolerating the odd mid-morning arrival when the au pair is sick; in Denmark it is expected that parents will arrive late or leave early a couple of days a week because they are taking their children to school or picking them up.

The reasons why Denmark has succeeded here where so many other countries have failed is, I believe, rooted in the country's egalitarianism (the reasons for that are fascinating, but not the subject of this book). But it seems to me that the concept of hygge must also be somewhere in the mix. Talk about hygge to any Dane and it soon becomes clear that spending time with the family is as hyggelig as it gets. It is far easier to be at the school gate on a regular basis, or to take your elderly parents out for tea every Wednesday, in a country whose working policies recognise the importance of life outside the office.

I have been lucky. Working freelance has meant that I have been able to develop an interesting career and be at home for the kids. I worked three full days while they were very small. This wasn't an economic decision since the work just about covered the nursery fees, but I knew I couldn't stay at home full time. Those working days enabled me to enjoy the quiet routines of duck-feeding and Lego-building with two preschool boys and gave me more patience to deal with the potty-training and the tantrums.

Once they went to school I fitted work around school hours, relying on an informal swapping arrangement with other mums and a willing granny when I had to be elsewhere at 3.30 p.m. Sometimes it was stressful; I hated those overrunning meetings when I had to choose between damaging my career by saying that I had to leave because I'd promised my children an ice cream on the common after school, and damaging the children by reneging on my promise. (In the end I usually managed both; leaving early but not early enough to avoid being too late for the ice cream van.) And in the days before email, I hated having to spend so many afternoons shushing my kids because I was always on the phone. But there were lots of lovely times too – hyggelige times, had I but known it. After-school walks to collect conkers in Richmond Park; teatimes spent reading them my favourite books – *Swallows and Amazons*, Kipling's *Just So Stories*, *The BFG* – and long summer holidays at the seaside. I would scoop them up straight from school on the last day of term and we'd be sitting on the slipway eating fish and chips two hours later.

My work hours grew as the boys did, and now that one has gone off to university and the other is doing his A levels I have no excuse to knock off halfway through the afternoon. I don't miss the stress of the morning packed-lunch-making, shoe-finding, book-bag-losing routine, and I do find my ability to schedule meetings at 4 p.m. quite liberating, but I miss those after-school times, and as the prospect of a totally empty nest looms, I find that I am distracting the still-at-home son just as he used to distract me. When he comes home from college, rather than leave him to his studies I'll suggest we go for a walk. Especially if the sun is shining. Before I discovered hygge, this habit made me feel guilty – guilty that I wasn't at my desk during office hours on a weekday afternoon and guilty that I was exhibiting such needy behaviour – but I have now learned to think of our regular tramps through the woods as precious hyggelige moments that are every bit as important as the emails in my inbox.

Hygge doesn't have a set of rules, but the Danes are clear about what does and does not facilitate its existence, and top of that list is the requirement for everyone involved in the activity to be totally present. That means not simultaneously posting pictures of themselves engaged in the activity on Instagram, talking to friends on social media or making mental lists of things to do when they get home. In second place comes the importance of acknowledging the hyggeness of the moment. My son and I do well on the first: he never takes his phone anywhere and I have learned to leave mine behind, so we are both mentally present. We talk, we comment on the scenery. However, we do fall short on the second requirement. I now name these walks as hyggelige, but he does not. For him they are just walks, pleasant enough and a good way of clearing his head before he goes back to his books, but not of any consequence. I am aware that, strictly speaking, this diminishes the hyggeness of our shared activity, but since we are not Danish and he has not signed up to my hygge experiment, the fact that he is eighteen and, from time to time, will still wander with me through woods filled with wild garlic is enough. I am claiming these outings as regular moments of hygge.

$$\wedge\!\vee\!\wedge$$

'The concept of hygge has family as its ultimate reference,' writes Jeppe Trolle Linnet in 'Money Can't Buy Me Hygge'.[16] He is right: the belief in the absolute sanctity of family life is the central core that runs through hygge, and, while I applaud the idea – I am, after all, a mother, sister and daughter with close ties to my children, brothers and parents – it also makes me wary. I can risk a migraine and cover my narrow wooden kitchen table with candles; I can embrace shared cooking, stop feeling guilty about eating cake and adopt a thirty-seven-hour working week that allows time off for plenty of hyggelige moments, but I can't do anything about the fact that my family does not fit the nuclear model of husband, wife and children that Jonathan Yorke Bean in his paper 'Consuming Hygge at Home' describes as being so strongly connected to the hygge ideal.[17]

I like to pretend that my two divorces have a certain Hollywood glamour, but, in truth, those two decrees absolute filed away at the bottom of the metal cabinet that doubles as my bedside table embarrass me. They are two certificates of failure. Rather than growing up in the cosy embrace of a nuclear family, my kids spent their childhoods ferrying their belongings from one parental home to another, and learned to think that two Christmases and birthday cake for breakfast every other year was entirely normal.

Divorce is all about loss. Of the partner you vowed to stay with until death did you part and, in most cases, a partial loss of any shared children, but also of your extended family. For me, divorce meant losing my in-laws, people I had come to love and now had no reason to know – particularly the second time around without a shared bloodline to bind us – and an end to family occasions with grandparents and uncles and cousins from both sides.

For a while I mourned all that loss with an intensity that brought on panic attacks, but time passes, as time does, and a couple of years ago, standing in the echo of my eldest son's bedroom a few hours after dropping him at his new student flat, I realised that I was happy again. He had grown and flown and still planned to come home from time to time, which seemed proof enough of a mothering job done. Not seamlessly, not without plenty of damaging errors, but passing well. My self-satisfaction lasted until my research into hygge brought me face to face with its deification of the nuclear family unit and I started to doubt myself all over again. Did my brace of divorces and the single-parent home I had made for the boys mean I was unable to lead a truly hyggelig life?

My first reaction was to wrap up all the candles I had bought in my recently acquired sofa blanket and chuck the whole lot in the bin. Then I took a look at the Danish divorce statistics. The figures for 2016 show that 54 per cent of marriages end in divorce, which is slightly more than in the UK.[18] Divorced families are such a common part of life that a Sunday evening train has apparently been named the 'divorce express', and a head teacher of a Danish school told a journalist writing for the *Guardian* newspaper that divorce is so widespread that 'it's not uncommon to hear a child say, "I heard you had Charles' father last year. I have him this year".'[19]

Reading this made me feel rather sorry for little Charles with his continually changing stepfamily, but the teacher's words also came as a relief. I took the prevalence of divorce in Denmark as proof that the Danes' understanding of family is broader than it initially appeared – either that, or a substantial section of the country's population is, like me, excluded from hygge's comforting embrace. The latter interpretation is possible, and certainly there are those who believe that hygge is a concept that alienates as many as it includes. (The anthropologist Linnet, for example, raises the suggestion that 'in spite of its egalitarian features, hygge acts as a vehicle for social control, establishes its own hierarchy of attitudes and implies a negative stereotyping of social groups who are perceived as unable to create hygge'.[20]) Persuasive as this argument is, when I discovered the high divorce rate I was looking for a way in to the hygge world, so I decided to go with the former explanation: blended families can be hyggelige too.

I grew up in a blended family. Not that we called them that then. Divorce was rarer in the late 1960s, and custody tended to go to mothers, with fathers being granted occasional visiting rights. For us that meant Dad turning up to eat Spaghetti Bolognese with us at Mum's house one Saturday every month. When we were old enough to be put on a train by ourselves, we went up to London and stayed for a weekend each half-term with Dad, his new wife and their son.

When my mother remarried, we acquired not only a stepfather but four stepsiblings too. We didn't see these three brothers and their sister much, but there was a blended holiday in Devon one summer. Six children all vying for their particular parent's attention. Looking back, it probably wasn't all that hyggelig, but that's family life for you.

My first holiday with my second husband and all four children wasn't very hyggelig either. Each separate family had their own routines, their own ways of being by the seaside, and resented any change. It didn't help that my boys and I were in my husband and his boys' house.

But there were lots of distinctly hyggelige times, too. Barbecues in a copse with my (ex) stepsons and their numerous cousins; intergenerational tennis matches. And, in my own childhood, a week every summer with my brother at our dad's wife's parents' house in Cornwall. There was a beach with rock pools large enough to swim in, a farm with cows that were milked by hand and two bonus grandparents who loved us as their own.

Extra relations are the one big advantage of second marriages and new partnerships – nobody can have too many people who care about them in their lives. My children have maintained relationships with all of their biological and inherited family, the cousins and stepcousins, the half-uncles and half-aunts, the several grandparents. I have not. Relations with my first husband's family were severed by our break-up; sides were taken out of hurt and protection. Geography and insufficient shared history mean that my second husband's family and I have little reason to keep in close touch.

No amount of good intentions is going to heal all the wounds, but my contemplations of hygge and family have made me determined to try and improve things. My first husband and I are now on friendly terms – he is happy with a new partner and Schadenfreude has played its part – and since that Christmas drink over the roast potatoes we have shared two birthday meals as a family. But his mother and I have been estranged for a decade.

A year ago, early on in my hygge experiment, she appeared on my deck. I walked out of the sliding doors and there she was, with ex-husband number one, waiting to pick up the boys. I was still sweaty from my morning run and taken by surprise, and I'm afraid my manners deserted me. I may even have said 'what are you doing here?'. Anyway, the encounter was over in a moment, and once I had recovered my equilibrium, I was ashamed at my most unhyggelig reaction, so I wrote her a letter to apologise. She wrote back, a conciliatory card understanding of my hostility, and we agreed to meet one time when she was visiting my ex-husband. Months went by and the meeting never happened – we were probably both wary – and then on Christmas Eve I bumped into her in the supermarket. Overcome with festive spontaneity, I invited her to tea. She arrived with the boys and both her sons (husband number one and his brother) and the six of us sat around the kitchen table eating mince pies for an hour or so. It was a small thing, and it made my Christmas. We have not met again since, but I am no longer concerned about meeting her by chance when she is staying in the village, and the knowledge that we could all celebrate some future milestone of the boys' lives together has reduced the sense of loss that I have felt ever since her son and I split up.

She did not come to my youngest son's eighteenth birthday lunch, although I did think about inviting her. Space dictated that I kept it to 'my side' of the family only, but even that required some blending. The guest list was the boys and I, plus the eldest's girlfriend and my boyfriend, my mother and her new partner, my brother, his wife and their two girls, my half-brother, my father and his wife. We have all got together before but, in the interval since we last met up, there have been a couple of rather unpleasant incidents. First, my full brother and I fell out in spectacular style – phones were thrown, swear words exchanged, impending visits cancelled – and then my father and my boyfriend had a political difference of opinion that turned nasty and personal. By the time of the party, the row with my brother had been resolved, more or less; the one between the other two men in my life had not, but, in the interests of hygge, I wanted to mark this significant birthday with a fully inclusive family event.

And I am glad I did. I cooked the Six-hour Lamb in wine recipe again and everyone pitched in. There was cake and, since I had recently read that no hygge event is complete without a bit of a sing-song, we sang. (We stopped at 'Happy Birthday', though, as we are British, not Danish.) I also decided to follow the unwritten but widely understood guidelines on suitably hyggelige topics of conversation.

During my research into the concept, time and again I have heard hygge described as being dependent upon a 'pleasant atmosphere' and, as many of the Danish people I have spoken to have explained, it is generally accepted that, when it comes to social gatherings, the best way to achieve this state of pleasantness is to avoid potentially contentious topics of conversation. This includes topics such as politics, religion, education and, no doubt, the lifestyle choices of certain members of the family. Adopting this non-confrontational approach at the birthday lunch meant that we talked about nothing of consequence, which made the conversation a little bland, but at least nobody got cross and spoiled the spirit of hygge. It was something of a compromise, and yes, I did have to make a conscious effort to keep the chat convivial, but that felt right for the occasion. It was my son's birthday and the people who love him had put aside their various differences to eat and drink in celebration.

Apparently, to admit that a traditionally hyggelig event such as Christmas, a family holiday or a birthday has not been hyggelig at all is an admission of real failure, and so many Danes go into denial. 'That was hyggelig,' they will say, to make it so in the family memory. Was this birthday lunch such an occasion? Possibly, for me. I was both silently furious at and saddened by my father's inability to speak to my boyfriend. I was aware that I trod more carefully around my brother than I used to, pre-row. But I was also genuinely pleased that we were all there together, and warmed by the sight of my family, blended and with bits missing as it is – no father of the birthday boy, only one set of grandparents, half the cousins – sitting elbow to elbow around my table. Was it a hundred per cent hyggelig? No, but if this exploration of what it is to live a more hyggelig life has taught me anything, then it is to stop feeling that I have failed and to enjoy things for what they are.

It has also caused me to reassess my attitude to conflict avoidance. I am opinionated and quick to temper. I believe that things are better confronted than supressed in the interests of the appearance of harmony. I used to rail against my paternal grandmother's insistence that we didn't upset Grandad by talking about politics or religion or the family's past. But I am tired of the loss that the last tumultuous decade has engendered, and now that the worst of the pain and the anger have subsided, I can see that perhaps there is some merit in putting a lid on the rest and pretending all is forgiven.

It is a realisation that led me, in the months following the birthday party, to privately extinguish a couple of persisting furies. The first with my father over his rejection of my boyfriend; the second with husband number two over his rejection of me. I say privately, because I didn't discuss my decision with either of them – that would have involved going over the reasons for my anger, something that would, I suspect, have relit the fires, since the embers are still pretty hot. I simply sent my dad a friendly email for no particular reason and finally accepted a long-standing invitation from ex number two to meet for a drink. The drink extended into supper in the end and, although there was a moment when the conversation turned to our past history and I was tempted to walk out, it passed and we parted at the tube station with a slightly awkward hug.

A few years ago I would have thought both these unspoken truces cowardly. I would have demanded either fully resolved peace or continuing war. But in my more temperate and slightly worn-out middle age, I can see that, in some circumstances, simply putting stuff aside and steering clear of topics of conversation that might lead to disagreement is an incredibly effective way of patching fences, and that while patched fences are imperfect, they are a whole lot better than broken ones.

I still enjoy a heated political spat over supper with friends, and I still believe in total honesty with those who share my intimate life, but when it comes to family – both current and former – I have decided to follow Granny's lead. I don't know whether the Danes feel that they are sweeping things under the carpet in order to create hygge; perhaps they really do have harmonious, issue-free families. But I doubt it – remember those divorce statistics? I think they are probably just better at acknowledging that sometimes the best route to contentment is down the path of least resistance.

# NO MAN IS AN ISLAND

Loneliness is bad for us. In 2006 a study by the University of California of three thousand women with breast cancer found that survival rates for those with a large circle of friends were four times higher than for those with fewer social connections. A year later, a team at the University of California Los Angeles discovered that the genes which regulate our immune response to cancer and the speed of tumour growth are switched on and off by social contact.[21]

These are extraordinary findings, and now that we can add yet another friend to our social circle at the touch of a screen, surely that should mean we are celebrating the end of loneliness and the consequent arrival of an era of unparalleled good health. But we are not. In fact, loneliness rates are on the rise. In 2013, a Campaign to End Loneliness survey estimated that there were around 800,000 chronically lonely people in England alone,[22] and in 2014, a study published by the Office for National Statistics found that the British and the Germans were the least likely of all Europeans to feel close to their neighbours.[23] Things are no better in the US where, according to the National Science Foundation's General Survey 2014, an 'unprecedented number of Americans' are now lonely.[24]

What these findings seem to suggest is that face-to-face contact matters. Five hundred Facebook friends you never meet do little to lessen the social isolation that is being facilitated by our ever-increasing ability to do everything we need to do from the solitary comfort of our armchairs. Rather than push our trolleys up and down the supermarket aisles where we might bump into a neighbour, we fill virtual baskets and interact with no one other than the delivery driver. Instead of meeting a colleague to discuss something, we send an email. We no longer watch a film in the shared space of a cinema auditorium; we stream it into our private realm. All this is very convenient, but it is shutting down our opportunities for social interaction and posing a risk to both our physical and mental health.

'Just as we all require food, water and sleep to survive,' wrote developmental psychologist and author Susan Pinker in an article in the *Guardian* newspaper in 2015, 'we all need genuine human contact. More socially cohesive societies – such as the Blue Zone of Sardinia – suggest that we should use our mobile devices to augment, not to replace, face-to-face interaction – that is if we want to live longer, healthier and happier lives.'[25]

The Danes are living lives that are no longer or healthier than the citizens of comparable nations, but if all those world happiness indexes are to be believed, they are leading happier ones. And one of the reasons for that seems to be their high level of social cohesion. Here are a few statistics. In 2010, 78 per cent of Danish people socialised with friends, family and colleagues at least once a week, compared with a European average of 60 per cent.[26] Ninety-five per cent of Danes reported having friends or relatives they could count on in times of trouble – that's 7 per cent more than the European average.[27] It is clear to me that those two things are connected: the Danes have strong social bonds because they make time for face-to-face interactions on a regular basis.

I work alone at the end of my garden. The lane runs several feet below my hut; if people do pass by, I do not see them. I also live by myself for the half of the week that my still-at-home son spends with his dad. (And, since he is about to head off to university, there will soon be nobody in the bungalow but me.) That means there are days when it is perfectly possible for me to see no one at all. I don't mind – I have always been content in my own company and I have a network of good friends and a boyfriend who I see regularly. I am close to my mother and my brother and his wife, and these are all people I can – and have – leaned on when times have been less than rosy. So while I am often solitary, I am not lonely.

What I have not been very good at are the looser acquaintances with work colleagues and neighbours. Other than a brief spell as an office temp, I have worked from home all my professional life; I have never acquired that habit of chatting around the water cooler and, though I live in a village, I don't do village life. I don't go to the community shop or the fete or the film night in the church hall. When the boys were small I would lurk at the periphery of the primary school playground at pick-up time and, while I am a member of the tennis club, I do not go to any club events.

This is partly down to a natural inclination towards unsociability and partly a side effect of the years I spent living in three places. When I left my first husband and met the man who was to become my second ex-husband, I withdrew from the few areas of village life that I had got involved in. I didn't like the sense that people I only knew from encounters in the shop or to arrange play dates with were familiar with the messy facts of my private life, and anyway, the plan was to move away as soon as the boys were through school. I saw my days at the rented cottage as precious, private time to spend with my children and began to focus my attention on building a sense of belonging in my new husband's homes in London and Dorset.

When the failure of that marriage meant leaving those homes, untying the social networks I had formed and moving back to Gloucestershire full time, it felt like an entirely new start. The bungalow is on the other side of the village from the rented cottage and further up the hill from the project/wreck I bought with my first husband, so it was new territory, and I didn't bother explaining to the neighbours that I had actually been in the village since 2003. If they knew I'd been here for over a decade, I reasoned, they'd wonder why I knew only a handful of people.

I wondered why I knew only a handful of people, but I didn't do anything about it until I embarked on the hygge experiment. My research led me to Copenhagen's Happiness Research Institute and their report 'The Happy Danes', published in 2014, that examines the reasons for Denmark's consistently high happiness ratings. The section on civil society opens with the following sentence: 'There is broad agreement among happiness researchers that social relations are essential for people's happiness . . . good neighbourly relations, participation in football – or stamp collecting clubs – all these things are good for happiness.'[28]

I have spent the last thirty-five years determinedly not participating in clubs of any kind. I blame this antipathy on my brief time as a Girl Guide, a movement I joined with the sole intention of going on the annual camp. (I was modelling myself on Nancy from *Swallows and Amazons* at the time and had romantic ideas about life under canvas.) The months leading up to camp were unhappy ones; the girls were bitchy and the meetings dull as we toiled away to gain badges in first aid and tea-making and then, when the big day finally came, I contracted German measles and had to be sent straight home. I hung up my navy nylon skirt and (badgeless) polyester shirt and turned my back on group activities of all kinds, until 'The Happy Danes' report forced me to reassess. It does not mention hygge specifically, but reading the chapter that looks at the reasons for Denmark's extraordinarily high levels of social cohesion, it was clear to me that the Danes' enthusiasm for engaging in a wide range of activities with family, friends and neighbours is linked to the pervasive culture of hygge. So I joined the local running club.

My first outing was not a success. We assembled early on a Tuesday evening at the local secondary school, where I was introduced to a largish group of Lycra-clad folk describing themselves as 'Faster Intermediates', who immediately set off to do 'efforts' along a nearby bicycle track. I knew about efforts – repeated bursts of intense speed separated by gentle recovery jogs – and had heard that they were the secret to becoming a faster runner, but I had never had the discipline to do them alone, so I was looking forward to it. The group was friendly, mostly around my age and nicely gender balanced. Our task was to effort down the track, a distance of about a mile, and recover back. Three times. I suppose I was keen to prove my credentials, which, coupled with an embarrassingly competitive streak, meant that I ran my fastest and finished the set in fifth place. This was a mistake. Being a non-joiner, I had no idea that protocol demands that new members, particularly female ones, under- rather than overplay their ability. Nobody said anything, but I sensed that I had been identified as a show-off.

The next outing was better. A long cross-country run at talking pace, it not only introduced me to the joys of off-road running, but also to the delights of running in company. I had never run with others before, and on that first Sunday-morning outing I discovered that there is real companionship to be found in keeping stride with someone as you make your way across beautiful countryside as the day begins. Two years on, these people have become my friends. They are not like the friends I have round for supper or go to exhibitions with; I don't meet them outside the club sessions and I have no idea what they look like when they're not wearing Lycra, but sweating up hills together and racing in the club colours has given us a bond.

Even more surprisingly, becoming a member of this club has given me a sense of belonging. The first time I ran the local half-marathon in a club vest somebody shouted 'come on, Stroud Lady' as I went past. It took me a moment to register that he was talking to me, and when I did, it dawned on me that by wearing this ill-fitting red, green and blue top, I had become part of my community. It was a small thing, but it filled me with a sense of contentment so deep that I glowed.

I haven't joined anything else – I am too fussy about what I read to submit to the unpredictable choices of a book group and I can't sing well enough to be part of a choir – but my avoidance is less pathological than it was. I am contemplating yoga, and only last week I went to a Surrealist quiz night at an artist's studio space in my local town that involved becoming part of a team. It was such good fun that I am tempted to do it again.

∧∨∧

Ultimately it is up to us whether or not we become part of a community. With its book groups and choirs, stitching circles and film nights, plus the community-run shop, my village offers more than enough opportunities for social interaction, so if I am often alone, it is by choice rather than force of circumstance. However, communities are not born; they have to be made. On a local level, this is the residents' job, but the physical layout of the area has a huge part to play too. Architects and urban planners can facilitate – or hamper – community engagement through the design of housing, roads, amenities and open spaces.

For much of the late twentieth century, urban and suburban development prioritised cars over people. People love their cars, and ownership boomed during the second half of the century, but the consequence of putting them first was the creation of endless anonymous housing estates bisected by roads so busy they cut neighbours off from one another, turned front gardens into drives and forced residents inside. Inhuman, dysfunctional places that encouraged social isolation.

Attitudes began to change as the new century dawned, and policymakers are now looking back to a time when the street was not simply a thoroughfare but a place for community interaction. 'Shared space' and 'placemaking' have become the new buzzwords in any discourse about housing and urban development. Fortunately, this is a worldwide phenomenon (exemplar communities filled with pedestrian streets and community gardens can be found everywhere from Britain to Canada via Amsterdam and Sweden), but Denmark is ahead of the curve. This is hardly a surprise given the country's human-centred approach to design, egalitarian outlook and, I would argue, hygge-embracing culture.

In 1967 the world's first co-housing project – or Bofaellesskaber (which literally translates as 'living community') – appeared on the outskirts of Copenhagen. Sættedammen was home to fifty families who had been inspired to build a new type of village by a newspaper article headed 'Children should have 100 Parents'. In it, journalist Bodil Graae set out the advantages of a more communal way of living – shared childcare, shared household chores (both pressing issues for the emerging generation of working wives and mothers) and better social cohesion. With its private houses, shared courtyards and community building for meals and meetings, Sættedammen was such a success that the idea spread across Denmark, out into the rest of Northern Europe and on to America. (The founders of co-housing in the United States were two architects, Kathryn McCamant and Charles Durrett, both of whom had studied architecture in Denmark.)

A decade later, the architectural practice Vandkunsten won a Ministry of Housing competition to build a new housing development in the town of Herfølge. Consisting of clusters of between twelve and seventeen apartments grouped around generous common facilities in a walkable environment, Tinggården was more in tune with the ideas of the co-housing movement than those of the Modernist architects. Small and intimate compared with the anonymity of high-rise tower blocks, it became the blueprint for residential architecture in Denmark. And its influence can be felt to this day; The Orient public housing scheme in Copenhagen, for example, which is due for completion in 2018, is similarly open and people-orientated, the architecture punctuated by plenty of open spaces and green terraces designed to invite community interaction.

This community-focused approach stretches beyond domestic housing projects and out into the public realm. In 1962, Copenhagen became the first city in the world to ban cars from a city centre street (Strøget), and the foremost architect in the field of human-centred urban design is a Dane with head offices in Copenhagen. Jan Gehl is driven by the belief that the starting point for all urban development should be the way people use a space (his 1971 book *Life Between Buildings* became a seminal text and has been reprinted many times), and that well-designed public space is fundamental to a successful society. 'In a society becoming steadily more privatised with private homes, cars, computers, offices and shopping malls,' he says, 'the public component of our lives is disappearing. It is more and more important to make the cities inviting so we can meet our fellow citizens face-to-face and experience directly through our senses.'

Copenhagen's Harbour Baths is perhaps the best example of this principle in action. Opened in 2002, the scheme transformed a harbour so polluted that it posed a risk to public health into an urban beach and free-to-use open-air water park. (It boasts five pools and three diving areas large enough to cater for more than six hundred people at a time.) The designer and placemaker Wayne Hemingway described it as 'the single greatest example of generous and intelligent design anywhere in the world'.[29] Come the Copenhagen summer, this is one of the most popular places in the city to go and indulge in some communal hygge.

In 2009, The Municipality of Copenhagen incorporated Jan Gehl's theories into a plan devised to turn Copenhagen into the world's most liveable city. The document, entitled 'A Metropolis for the People', which sets out the aims of the plan, states: 'a varied urban life is an important part of a socially sustainable city. We meet people in the city's common spaces. A short chat on a bench or just eye contact – these are what give us quality of life and increase our understanding of each other.'[30]

'A Metropolis for the People' had three major goals: More Urban Life for All; More People to Walk More and More People to Stay Longer.[31] It promised to 'create more urban life for everybody with a variety of urban space and activities twenty-four hours a day all the year round', and to 'create squares, parks, streets and waterside quays which invite more people to stay there longer – both in the city centre, in new urban areas as well as where we live and go around on a daily basis'. It encouraged people to walk more not only because of the health benefits, both to Copenhageners and the environment, but also because it 'offers us the opportunity  to meet other people'.

Copenhagen duly won its gong; *Monocle* magazine awarded it the number one spot on its list of the world's Top 25 Most Liveable Cities in both 2013 and 2014. 2014 also saw the government launch a National Architecture Policy for Denmark which made a 'people first' approach to architecture a national political goal. (So no one misses the point, the policy document is called 'Putting People First'.[32]) Launching the policy, the Minister of Culture Marianne Jelved said, 'We will build for people. We will develop cities and places where it is pleasant to be, where we can meet [each other] in pleasant, inspiring surroundings.'[33]

What I find remarkable about both that statement and the goals set out in 'A Metropolis for the People' is their attention to human scale. It is true that the latter was devised to help Copenhagen win the World's Most Liveable City award, but pocket parks and more benches are hardly the headline-grabbing goals of a city more focused on prizes than on its people. These plans recognise that however sophisticated our cities, however filled with WiFi hotspots and twenty-four-hour commerce, however thrusting, what really matters is face-to-face social contact. Just as it always has. Making that a national policy seems to me to be a sign of a country with its priorities in the right place. (I am sad to discover that Britain has no such policy. In 2014 the Royal Institute of British Architects published a report calling for a national, long-term architectural policy similar to Denmark's, but as I write this, nothing has happened. No British city has even made it on to *Monocle*'s Liveable City list.) Creating people-friendly public spaces is not hygge in itself, and it is true that most hyggelige activities take place in private homes, but I do think that it is deeply hyggelig to cater for people's need for human interaction and provide public spaces in which to relax.

Odense, Denmark's third-largest metropolis, has recently transformed itself from a struggling, post-industrial city into a place that is both thriving and liveable. Cars have been squeezed out to the edges, channelled into a park-and-ride system on the outskirts or down into subterranean car parks, and much of the four-lane highway that cuts across the city has been turned over to bicycles and pedestrians. The city boasts 120 parks and 250 playgrounds. Its new motto is 'At leger er at leve' – to live is to play. If that's not hygge, I don't know what is.

'*Making food together is a special experience which can be categorised as hyggelig. It is very important that you are not pressed for time or other circumstances that may force you to hurry up. You may open a bottle of wine and share a glass with your partner – and if you have adult children then also with them. If you have smaller children, you may ask them to prepare an alcohol-free drink themselves. While you are all working on your dinner together, you talk and joke with each other. When you sit down to eat, you continue to go slowly – there are no deadlines. We do this quite often on a Friday or Saturday evening, and it is fantastic and very hyggelig*'

# HOW TO HYGGE:
## LIVING

# ENTERTAINING HYGGE-STYLE

Eating with friends and family is the epitome of hygge, especially at Christmas which, with its focus on home-based family time coupled with the need for twinkling lights and open fires, is the ultimate hyggelig event. I'm sure there are plenty of Danes who wear themselves out preparing for a dinner party, or wake in the night worrying about whether they remembered to buy almonds to hide in the Risalamande (concealing an almond in rice pudding is the Danish equivalent of putting a coin in the plum pudding), but in theory, entertaining hygge-style is relaxed, sociable and totally stress-free. Here's how:

**Share the workload.** Someone has to provide the venue, but everyone can bring a dish. Alternatively, ask people to bring raw ingredients and turn the cooking into a group activity. Open a bottle, put on some music, light the candles and make the preparation a hyggelig event in itself.

**Keep the food simple.** Christmas brings its own menu – in Denmark that most often means roast pork; roast duck stuffed with apples and prunes; boiled potatoes, caramelised potatoes and red cabbage followed by Risalamande and a marzipan pig for the lucky finder of the almond. For other gatherings, think slow-cooked, one-pot dishes that fill the room with appetising smells and require minimal intervention. Start with good-quality ingredients and let the natural flavours speak for themselves. And stay in your comfort zone. If you can only do one dish, do that and make it your signature.

**Don't pander to the whims of your guests.** This might not sound like hygge, but I was interested to discover that because hygge requires everyone's full and equal participation, fussy food preferences are rather frowned upon.

For her PhD thesis 'Food and Health in Late Modernity: An Insight into Hygge and Related Food Practices', Heidi Boye carried out a series of in-depth interviews. Her research revealed that, while food allergies were tolerated, refusing to eat the Brunede Kartofler (caramelised potatoes), for example, because you are cutting out carbs, would be considered unhyggelig in the extreme.[34]

It's a tricky one – forcing someone to eat something they hate doesn't seem very hyggelig, either – but having recently cooked for a group that included a coeliac, someone who 'felt more energised' by not eating dairy and another convinced that tomatoes increased the risk of early-onset arthritis, I can certainly vouch for the stress that twenty-first century food angst can cause. My solution? Don't ask about food intolerances – if someone has an allergy or a serious objection to a certain food, I'm sure they will tell you.

**Forget formality.** The table setting should be as understated as the food. In the English summary of her dissertation, Heidi Boye states that one of the elements that does not contribute to hygge is 'nice crockery'.[35] I don't think this is a call to serve Christmas lunch on paper plates, but it is a reminder that you don't need to worry about digging out the easily chipped matching dinner service you inherited from a great-aunt and which won't go in the dishwasher.

**Take it slowly.** Meals with the people you care about should be savoured, so slow down and take your time. Put your phones away.

# HYGGE FOOD

Hygge is about comfort. Food-wise that means dishes that nourish both body and spirit and which speak of home. For a Dane that may well be Frikadelle, a dish of pork, potatoes and preserved sour vegetables in a thick brown sauce, or a stjerneskud smørrebrød (shooting star open sandwich) with its layers of buttered rugbrød (rye bread), battered plaice fillets, steamed fish, shrimps, remoulade (black or red caviar), lemon, salmon, asparagus, cucumber, tomato, lettuce, hard-boiled egg and dill. And for dessert perhaps a bowl of rødgrød med fløde, a red berry pudding with cream. But really, as the people at Snaps and Rye explained, there are no specific hyggelig foods and anyway, this is not a cookery book, so, rather than recipes, what follows here are some suggestions as to what a more hyggelig approach to food can do for the soul.

**Enjoy what you eat.** Guilt has no place at the table, so banish all thoughts of 'good' and 'bad', 'clean' and 'dirty'. Yes, some foods are healthier than others and we should all try and make sure that the former outweigh the latter in our daily diet, but carbohydrates are not the work of the devil and there is much pleasure to be had from eating a bowl of cream-rich pasta or a slice of cake. Buy the best-quality ingredients you can afford, pay heed to animal welfare and air miles (knowing your food isn't damaging the planet will make you feel good) and cook it well.

**Take your time.** Food is much more than fuel. However simple the meal, make time to sit down and savour the moment. Select tableware that pleases the eye and feels good to the touch. If it can go in the dishwasher too, so much the better. If not, put some music on and wash up with those who shared your meal.

**A little bit of what you fancy does you good.** There is nothing excessive about hygge. That may sound dull, but the great thing about moderation is that you can't overdo it. And if you can't overdo it, you don't need to detox. Say goodbye to Dry January.

**Make some edible, smellable signs of home.** Nothing says home quite like the smell of baking and the sight of jars full of preserves. You don't have to do anything complicated – remember, one of the wonderful things about hygge is that it is anti-showing off, so forget fancy icing and embrace that slightly soggy bottom on your cake. Having food on display – a bowl full of fruit on the table, a line of storage jars on an open shelf or a basket of vegetables on the kitchen worktop, for example – will also help to create a sense of home.

**Observe your traditions – and create some new ones.** Family traditions are very hyggelige and food has the power to evoke memories like little else – just think of Proust and his madeleines. Dig out your grandmother's recipes; start cooking with your kids; mark all the high days of the year with a feast. And if you want to bring a really Danish flavour to your new traditions, you could try baking a batch of honninghjerter (honey hearts) at the start of December, or some kransekage (almond cookies) for New Year's Eve. And ginger biscuits. The Danes love a ginger biscuit.

**Give your guests cake.** Seeing your friends is a cause for celebration, and celebrations are always more joyous with cake.

# HYGGE WITH FRIENDS
# AND FAMILY

The whole concept of hygge centres around time spent with family and close friends. No one would claim that the Danes have found the solution to perfect family life (the high divorce rate is evidence enough of that), but the principles of hygge do offer a pretty good template. These are the key points.

**Make time.** The Danes' relatively short working week and long holidays do mean that they have more leisure time than many people elsewhere in the world. But time is about priorities. The Danes make time for frequent get-togethers with friends and family because they think these relationships are an important part of life. Set aside a couple of evenings each week to have supper with your children; make Wednesday night Friends Night; try having lunch with your work colleagues once a week. (Many Danish offices have synchronised lunchtimes so that everyone can eat together.) Timetabling your life might not be very spontaneous, but it does mean that you see the people who matter to you on a regular basis.

**Keep the conversation harmonious.** 'Consensus is important [in hyggelige times],' writes Heidi Boye in the English summary of her thesis, 'and this may require avoiding discussion of sensitive topics like politics, religion, the economy and the raising of children.'[36] There's nothing my children and friends like more than a heated debate, but there's a fine line between debate and argument and the latter will destroy hygge in an instant. The artist Grayson Perry was channelling hygge when he named one of his tapestries *Hold your Beliefs Lightly*.

**Contribute.** Hygge is about everyone doing their bit, not just in practical terms but also socially and emotionally. Again and again in my research I heard people speak about how important it was for everyone to take an equal part in the conversation or activity; to be mentally present. A family movie night is not hygge if half the people on the sofa are Snapchatting with their friends, so when you are having a hygge moment, ask everyone involved to put their phones somewhere out of reach.

**But don't overdo it.** Hygge is egalitarian. No one should take centre stage at a hyggelig gathering.

# HYGGE IN THE COMMUNITY

Almost half of all households in Denmark are occupied by a single person (47.4 per cent in 2013 according to Eurostat People in the EU Statistics on Household and Family Structures),[37] yet the Danes apparently feel less lonely and better supported than the citizens of most other OECD countries. Hygge can't take all the credit for this happy state of affairs, but the fact that getting together with your local community is considered to be a hyggelig activity must surely play a part. In the interest of hygge and happiness, here are some things to try.

**Get to know the locals.** The co-housing movement originated in Denmark in the late 1960s. Sættedammen, on the outskirts of Copenhagen, was home to fifty families who lived in their own houses but who shared gardens and frequently cooked together in a common house. Communal living, with its emphasis on equal participation and the sharing of chores is very hygge, but it is perfectly possible to foster hyggelige relations with your neighbours without actually moving in with them. Say hello when you pass them in the street; invite them to drinks at Christmas; suggest a babysitting swap; meet for cake once a month – it doesn't matter what it is as long as you make a connection. You may not have much in common, but you do share the same geographical space and that is a bond worth nurturing.

**Make the most of public spaces.** There is a generosity of public open space in Denmark, which is surprising for a country that has a less-than-inviting climate. Summertime sees Danes flocking to outdoor areas such as Copenhagen's Harbour Baths, a free, open-all-hours urban beach with multiple swimming pools. Or Nørrebro Park, an impressive urban green space conceived as a series of different areas to appeal to a diverse range of visitors. There are two pavilions for small concerts and markets, for example, along with a beach volleyball pitch, a rose garden, skateboard ramps and avenues of linden trees. Outdoor events are popular too – according to the report 'The Urban Life Account: Trends in Copenhagen's Urban Life 2013', 73 per cent of Copenhageners said that they took part in, or were spectators at, an event in the urban space at least a couple of times a year. Of this group, 29 per cent said that they take part in events at least once a month.[38]

And they don't all rush indoors in winter. There may be lots of hygge at home, but city-living Danes still walk and cycle everywhere (80 per cent of movements in inner-city Copenhagen are on foot, while Odense boasts 350 miles of bicycle lanes); they still go to the parks and the Harbour Baths and, according to The Urban Life Account survey, 37 per cent of Copenhageners still sit outdoors in cafés and restaurants at least once a week.

As I have already set out, much of this is down to the country's approach to designing public space, but it is also about individuals making a choice to go out into the community regardless of the weather. Assuming your local planning department has had the good sense and humanity to create a pocket park or pedestrianised square somewhere nearby (or to leave the village green undeveloped), then make an effort to use it. Take a blanket and a book on a

summer afternoon, or go and eat your lunchtime sandwich on a bench. You don't have to speak to anyone; just being in a local space will connect you to your neighbourhood. But if you really want to do the community thing, you could organise a picnic or a game of rounders. And in winter, do the same; just take a big coat and a flask of something warming.

If you are unfortunate enough to live somewhere without any shared public space, then go to your local council offices and complain until someone does something about it.

**Join a club.** The Danes love clubs so much that there is even a saying, 'when three Danes meet, they form a club'. And they are on to something: not only is there pleasurable companionship to be found in doing something that interests you in the company of others who share your passion, but, according to Susan Pinker's fascinating book *The Village Effect: Why Face-to-Face Contact Matters*, being part of a group is also vital for our health. 'Living in a community is so essential to survival,' she writes, 'that an early warning system evolved that rings biochemical alarm bells when we are ostracised.'[39]

**Volunteer.** International happiness researchers suggest that there is a close link between participation in voluntary work and levels of personal happiness. Thirty-five per cent of Danes aged over sixteen reportedly do some kind of voluntary work each year – that's more than any other country in Europe according to a Quality of Life Survey carried out in 2011 – and their country is, yet again, top of the world happiness tables.[40] It's not just the warm glow cast by a shining halo that makes us happy, either; volunteering also helps to strengthen social relations, without which we can feel isolated and lonely. Apparently we are more likely to sustain our involvement if we choose a cause we feel strongly about and keep our activities local.

I must confess that, to date, my volunteering record is poor. For a few years I spent an hour every Wednesday morning listening to the infants read at my children's primary school, and recently I put on a high-vis vest and acted as a marshal at my running club's annual half-marathon. These are lowly forays into the vounteering world, but both have been enormously rewarding. I was delighted when I helped young Molly or Ben decipher a difficult word, and I found that three hours spent setting out cones and cheering on runners as they reached the top of the longest hill in the race deepened my sense of belonging both to the club and to the wider community of runners. Now that I have more or less given up racing myself, I will definitely be doing it again.

**Nurture your social interactions.**  Our social connections matter – loneliness has been identified as a risk factor for early death – so it is vital that we make time to look after them. Rather than thinking of lunch with a work colleague or coffee with a neighbour on a Sunday morning as an indulgence to be enjoyed only when there's nothing else pressing (which means it never happens), prioritise these connections as you would any other health-enhancing activity. And if that means the ironing doesn't get done, then so be it: nobody died of a creased shirt. Or, if you're really pressed for time, try making things you already do more sociable: join the local running club, or set up an office yoga class. Garden with a friend. I don't know whether housework clubs are already a thing, but they could be. Communal vacuuming, anybody?

'Returning from a long business trip and
feeling that the family has missed me and are now
enjoying being with me and listening to what I have
experienced; finding myself at my home where
I feel free and safe and am surrounded by natural
materials; when my pulse gets back to normal
and I have a craving to sleep – all this is hygge'

# HYGGE
# FOR THE
# SOUL

# THE SERIOUS BUSINESS
# OF HAPPINESS

Denmark is as famous for its happiness as it is for its pastries. Type the words 'Denmark' and 'happiness' into Google and you will be rewarded with link after link to articles about this most southerly of the Nordic countries being home to the happiest people on earth. And, lest anyone try to dismiss it as nothing more than media hype, there is plenty of official certification to support the Danes' claim. The country came top of the inaugural World Happiness Report in 2012, repeating the feat in both 2013 and 2014. It was briefly knocked off its pedestal by Switzerland in 2015, but swiftly regained the title of the world's happiest nation the following year. Coming from the UK, which has yet to make it into the Top 20 (the 2016 report placed the UK at number 23), I can only look on in – slightly sour – awe.

I was overfamiliar with all the statistics when I arrived in Copenhagen one Friday morning in February. It was rush hour. Sitting on the metro heading through the suburbs towards the city centre, the only thing that really struck me as being in any way remarkable was the fact that I could sit down. Otherwise my fellow passengers, hunched into their puffy winter coats and intent on their phones, were as weary-looking and closed off to their immediate surroundings as any other commuter in any other city I have visited.

The people we encountered over the course of our stay smiled at us politely, and I did notice that that they seemed quite content to be riding their bicycles despite the persistent horizontal sleet, but no one seemed exactly overcome by a surfeit of merriment. Except for the revellers we found in a bar one Saturday night. Everyone in this hot and smoke-filled place (it was one of several public spaces small enough to be exempt from the smoking ban) was full of beery bonhomie, including the large group of young men who, rather than growing increasingly pugnacious with every pint, simply hugged each other more and more frequently before finally passing out.

I returned home feeling a little disappointed. The Danes are so much further up the happiness scale than we Brits that I had assumed I would notice the difference. That's the trouble with overdosing on newspaper articles headed 'the happiest people on earth'; they lead you to expect laughing Danes on every street corner and candlelit groups singing on the bus. The experience made me wonder what exactly those happiness reports mean when they describe a nation's people as 'happy'.

The nature of happiness has been a subject of philosophical discussion for millennia. In the third century BC, the Chinese philosopher Zhuangzi wrote *The Tao of Perfect Happiness*, the second major text of the Taoist tradition. He claimed that happiness was man's ultimate goal in life and divided it into two kinds: the craving for material possessions and the desire for more internal things, thus laying the foundations for our understanding of happiness ever since.

The Greek philosopher Aristotle was an approximate contemporary of Zhuangzi. Aristotle is generally regarded as the man who introduced the world to the idea of a science of happiness and, certainly, he devoted more space to the contemplation of the nature of happiness than any other thinker of his time, setting out his theories in his work *Nicomachean Ethics*.

I am no classical scholar, but as far as I understand it, Aristotle shared Zhuangzi's belief that happiness was the ultimate goal of human existence. 'Happiness,' he wrote, 'is the meaning and the purpose of life, the whole aim and end of human existence.' Again like Zhuangzi, he saw a distinct difference between mere gratification and inner happiness. For Aristotle, true happiness, or 'eudaimonia' in Greek, was not a temporary state of joy that could be reached through the pursuit of pleasure: '. . . it is not one day or a brief time that makes a man blessed and happy,' he said. That kind of happiness was for the animals, simple beasts at the mercy of their physical urges. Humans should strive for an altogether higher and more permanent sort of happiness, one entirely dependent upon the exercise of reason and the cultivation of virtue. (These virtues of Courage, Citizenship, Generosity, Justice and Friendship could be achieved by maintaining a balance – or 'mean' – between the extremes of excess and deficiency. Courage, for example, is the mean between the excess of recklessness and the deficiency of temerity.) What's more, since happiness depended on the totality of a person's life, it could only be properly assessed when that life came to an end. I think it's safe to assume that Aristotle would have given the Danes' happiness ratings short shrift, since they are based on a questionnaire that required respondents to rate their current state of overall happiness on a scale of nought to ten.

A slightly different view was offered by another Greek philosopher, Epicurus. Born on the island of Samos forty or so years after Aristotle, he too was exercised by the question of what makes for a happy life. Epicurus believed that all human actions were driven by the pursuit of pleasure and the avoidance of pain. His proposal that 'hedone', or pleasure, was the most important factor in determining a person's happiness has meant that he has gone down in history as an advocate of instant gratification; a pusher of seductive, but ultimately hollow, hedonism. However, it seems to me that his philosophy was closer to Aristotle's slower, more internal form of happiness than it might seem at first glance. (And in 'From the Happiness of Virtue to the Virtue of Happiness 400 B.C.–A.D. 1780', Darrin M. McMahon, Professor of History at Dartmouth College, describes him as 'an unimpeachable ascetic who taught that "genuine pleasure" was not "the pleasure of profligates", but rather the simple satisfaction of a mind and body at peace'.[1])

Epicurus' view was that pleasure was nothing more than the absence of pain, in both the body and the soul. He argued that a tranquil mind and a pain-free body produced a state of static pleasure which could legitimately be described as 'happiness'. Pursuing pleasure beyond this static state, on the other hand, was an entirely fruitless endeavour that risked increasing a person's desires with most unhappy results. 'The presence of wealth, honour and admiration among the many will not produce joy or dissolve the disturbance of the soul,' he advised. 'Living a quiet life among like-minded friends will more likely lead to the happy life.'[2]

Compared with hedonism, eudaimonia and static pleasure don't sound terribly exciting and, once upon an eighties nightclubbing time, I would rather have cut up my dancing shoes than embrace that kind of quiet contentedness. But while no one other than the Puritans and the most fundamental of fundamentalists disputes our need for a bit of full-on, sugar-rush pleasure, what the current wave of happiness research is revealing, as Zhuangzi, Aristotle and Epicurus all maintained, is that the secret to true and lasting happiness depends on a whole lot more than mere sensual gratification.

According to the annual World Happiness Report, which is generally regarded as something of a gold standard in the happiness measuring field, happiness depends upon six factors: Gross Domestic Product (GDP) per capita, healthy years of life expectancy, social support (measured by having someone to count on in times of trouble), trust (measured by a perceived absence of corruption in government and business), generosity (measured by recent donations) and perceived freedom to make life decisions. Each of these factors is measured with a population-weighted average score on a scale running from nought to ten, which is tracked over time and compared against the other countries in the survey.

Given those criteria, it is hardly surprising that Denmark and other small, wealthy Western European countries with high levels of welfare such as Sweden, Norway, Switzerland and the Netherlands consistently top the charts. What they don't do, however, is cast any light on why Denmark almost always does better than its equally socially aware, democratic and affluent neighbours. In an attempt to understand the Danish secret, The Happiness Research Institute decided to carry out its own study. The resulting report, 'The Happy Danes', included the results of a survey of 10,000 Danish citizens who were asked questions relating to each of the World Happiness Report variables in turn.

It makes fascinating reading. When it came to trust, for example, it turns out that not only do the Danes trust their government, they also trust each other. Three out of four people said they believed that they could trust friends and strangers alike – that's a world record. And while I may not have come across any singing Danes during my visit to Copenhagen, I did see plenty of evidence of mutual trust. Parents leave their children sleeping in their pushchairs outside shops and cafés; bicycles are left unlocked. The authors of the report argue that there are two reasons why this adds to the happiness of a nation.

It makes life easier on a practical level (it is much simpler to leave baby Lars out on the street while you pop into the post office, rather than struggle to navigate the pushchair through a revolving door), and it also creates the comforting feeling that our fellow citizens are on our side. 'What is really valuable,' the report states, 'is the joy of being able to trust one another and the sense that our fellow human beings wish us well. This is one of the factors which makes Denmark happy.'[3]

There is more to the GDP question than first appears, too. It is undoubtedly true that rich countries are happier than poor ones and several surveys, including the one carried out for 'The Happy Danes' report and a far bigger 'European Social Survey', have shown that there is an increase in happiness for every step up a person takes on the household income ladder.[4] However, while Denmark and the other countries in the top five are certainly extremely wealthy, there are plenty of equally rich ones further down the list – the US is currently ranked at number thirteen, for example, and there has been no increase in the happiness of the British or the Americans since the mid-1950s, despite a dramatic increase in the national wealth of both countries.

This seems to be due to two things. The first is that once our basic needs have been met, the quality of our social relations becomes the most important factor in our happiness. ('The Happy Danes' report cites data from a Danica Pensions happiness survey showing that people who were most satisfied with their relationships scored an average of 8.4 on the happiness scale, while those who were the least satisfied scored 4.5 – a difference of four points. The difference in happiness between the lowest and highest incomes in contrast was 0.5.)

The second is inequality. 'The Happy Danes' refers to OECD data from the Better Life Index (which measures life satisfaction, among other things, in thirty-six different countries) showing that when people experience significant and systematic differences in living conditions and between social class, gender and ethnic groups, it has a negative effect on their sense of happiness. Denmark's generous welfare state means that there is greater equality between rich and poor. The happiness surveys reveal that the less well-off are happier in Denmark than they are anywhere else in the world, and that this relatively small number of unhappy people is a key factor in the country's high rankings in the happiness charts. As Andrew Oswald, Professor of Economics at the University of Warwick, puts it, 'Denmark is good at preventing extreme unhappiness.'[5]

It seems clear to me that the practical factors responsible for Denmark's low levels of reported unhappiness are the same as those for its happiness – good welfare, trust in others and a well-functioning government and civil society. But I would also suggest that it is possible that they do well on both counts because they recognise that taking happiness seriously means that they must address unhappiness. Take their record on mental health. Lots of the articles about Denmark's status as the world's happiest nation cite the high levels of anti-depressant usage – 35 per cent higher than the OECD average – as an indicator that perhaps all is not quite as wonderful in the country as it seems. This is a very complex area, and I couldn't find any statistics about the Danish mental health system's use of talking therapies, but when I asked Meik Wiking, CEO of The Happiness Research Institute, about the anti-depressant statistics, he made an interesting point. 'One of the reasons we do well on world happiness indexes,' he said, 'is because of our welfare state. That same welfare state recognises mental illness and tries to remedy it. We don't have a high suicide rate – the countries with the lowest consumption of anti-depressants have high suicide rates.'

It was widely accepted that governments should give due consideration to the happiness – and unhappiness – of their people right up until the latter end of the nineteenth century. America's Founding Father Thomas Jefferson, who famously incorporated 'the pursuit of happiness' into the American Declaration of Independence in 1776 (the phrase had initially been used by the English Enlightenment thinker John Locke), asserted that 'the care of human life and happiness is the only legitimate objective of good government'. In eighteenth-century Italy, economists made 'pubblica felicità' – public happiness – the motto for their new science, while in Britain the philosopher Jeremy Bentham gave birth to Utilitarianism, an ethical system with the principle of 'the greatest good for the greatest number' at its heart. His ideas were subsequently echoed by another Briton, the philosopher and political economist John Stuart Mill.

It was the triumph of capitalism at the turn of the century which caused Western nations, in particular, to turn their backs on the subjective notion of happiness as a mark of progress in favour of that thoroughly objective measure, Gross Domestic Product. (It's interesting to note, however, that the creator of free market economics, Scottish philosopher Adam Smith, chose to call his seminal book *An Enquiry into the Nature and Causes of the Wealth of Nations*. The word 'wealth' comes from 'weal' meaning well-being, prosperity, individual and collective happiness, suggesting that perhaps Smith believed a nation's richness was more than simply the value of its material goods.)

There were some notable twentieth-century exceptions to the 'GDP rules' approach. On 18 March 1968, for example, US presidential hopeful Bobby Kennedy made a speech at an election rally at the University of Kansas in which he asserted, 'Gross National Product does not allow for the health of our children, the quality of their education, or the joy of their play. It does not include the beauty of our poetry or the strength of our marriages; the intelligence of our public debate or the integrity of our public officials . . . it measures everything, in short, except that which makes life worthwhile.' And in 1971, Bhutan replaced Gross National Product with Gross National Happiness as a measure of its success.

But it wasn't until the second decade of the twenty-first century that happiness returned as a subject of urgent interest to social scientists, psychologists and, crucially, economists and politicians.

In the year 2000, happiness data existed for 78 nations; the 2016 World Happiness Report surveyed 156 countries. In 2010, the then British Prime Minister David Cameron announced: 'We will start measuring our progress as a country not just by how our economy is growing, but by how our lives are improving; not just by our standard of living, but by the quality of life.' A year later, three economic and academic heavyweights – Lord Richard Layard, Professor of Economics at the LSE and founder-director of the Centre of Economic Performance, Sir Anthony Seldon, Vice-Chairman of Buckingham University and Geoff Mulgan, Chief Executive of NESTA and co-founder of the think tank Demos – launched a national body committed to building a happier, more caring society called Action for Happiness. Then on 2 April 2012 the inaugural World Happiness Report was published and the United Nations held its first conference on happiness and well-being at its headquarters in New York.

Entitled 'Wellbeing and Happiness: Defining a New Economic Paradigm', the conference built on a UN General Assembly resolution proposed by the Prime Minister of Bhutan and agreed in July 2011 encouraging countries to promote the happiness of their citizens. All proof that, as the opening paragraph of the 2016 World Happiness Report Update states, 'It is now widely accepted that happiness is a proper measure of social progress and should be the goal of social policy.'[6]

Much of the political interest comes down to the realisation that happy people are better for society and the economy. Happy people are likely to earn more – academics from University College London and Warwick University analysed data from 15,000 adolescents and young adults in the US and found that a one-point increase in life satisfaction at the age of twenty-two is associated with almost two thousand dollars more in annual earnings by the age of twenty-nine.[7] Happy people are more likely to volunteer and participate in the democratic process, and they are likely to cost the country less because they tend to be healthier. Happy people have been shown to have lower blood pressure, better immune systems, fewer aches and pains and even live longer lives.

In perhaps the most famous study of happiness and longevity, the life expectancy of Catholic nuns was linked to the amount of positive emotion they expressed in an autobiographical essay they were asked to write when they first entered their convent.[8] Researchers examined their manuscripts looking for expressions of positive feelings such as amusement, contentment, gratitude and love. The results revealed that those who had written the happiest essays lived between seven and ten years longer than those who had written the least happy.

Politicians may only be interested in the well-being of the people they govern because it means higher productivity, more engaged citizens and less ill health, but their motivation doesn't matter. What does matter is that they are talking about it, and that it is now widely accepted that happiness is important on both an individual and a societal level. Which brings us back to Denmark and, in my opinion, the deep-rooted culture of hygge.

Hygge does not feature as a variable in any of the surveys or happiness studies (how could it when it is unique to Denmark?) but, despite that, I believe it plays as important a role as any of the official measures. Hygge is ingrained in Danish culture; it is part of what it is to be a Dane, so if you are Danish, paying attention to your well-being is likely to be part of the routine of your life; happiness is a concept that you are probably comfortable thinking about. At the very least, that means the Danes are better placed than other nationalities to answer vague and subjective questions such as 'how happy are you overall?'.

Nor does hygge align itself with any of the theories of happiness – and none of the Danes I have spoken to claim that it should. But I can see plenty of overlap. It seems to me, hygge tourist that I am, that the key tenets of the concept – meaningful time spent in the company of family and friends, the absence of anything excessive and, to quote anthropologist Judith Friedman Hansen, a 'readiness to commit oneself to the experience of the moment'[9] – have much in common with happiness science both ancient and modern. I can certainly hear echoes of Epicurus' advice about happiness being found in a 'modest life lived among friends'.

# RAISING THE WHITE FLAG

Shortly after I discovered hygge, a writing project came through that took over my life. The final few weeks before it was due to be delivered were ones of fervent industry. I woke early each morning with my head full of the previous day's phrases and the coming day's word count, having dreamed of missed deadlines and computer failures. The season changed; the move from spring to summer, marked by the ceremonial coiling away of the wire for the hut's plug-in radiator and, a couple of weeks later, the throwing open of its double doors, leaving my ordered piles of research notes at the mercy of the wind. Weekdays merged unnoticed into weekends. Fortunately, the still-at-home son was studying for exams at the same time, so my neglect of him went unnoticed and the two of us would meet over supper, then collapse on the sofa in front of the telly for an hour of convivial mindlessness before bed. There was an urgency and purpose to it all that I found stimulating, but one Sunday in late May I woke up exhausted.

The alarm went at seven o'clock as it always does on a Sunday so that I can run with the club but, despite the unblemished blueness of the sky, the singing of the birds and the promise of companionable running though bucolic glades filled with cow parsley and buttercups, I could not bring myself to leave my bed. I slept again, and when I woke at nine my pleasure at having slept so late was tempered by the nag in my head that told me I should be up and running. Seizing rather than idling away the hours ahead.

I shared my sense of my guilt with my boyfriend, who laughed at my mania and went back to sleep. Envious of his lack of obligation to the coming day, I made a decision to take a day off, not just from running but from everything. No work, no chores. I was going to hygge myself. (The fact that I could justify this in the interests of research went some way to satisfying that inner puritan nag. As did my plan to get up extra early the next day in order to fit in a really long run to compensate for my laziness.)

I began by reading in bed for another hour, curled against the boyfriend's slumbering form. It was a casual coming together, both heedless and deeply sensual, and I realised what I missed by leaping out of bed the moment my phone announced the morning. It is relatively easy to make time for sex, particularly if you stop familiarity spreading its complacency by not living full time with your partner, but this kind of low-level lovemaking is a slow thing, its delights less tangible, and it can get lost in life's rush.

I haven't come across very many discussions of hygge sex (when I typed the phrase into Google, I was asked if I meant 'huge sex'; I did not), but the Danish people's response to an online marketing video posted by Visit Denmark in 2009 is illuminating. In the film, Karen – who is, unsurprisingly, young, attractive and blonde – is attempting to trace a man she spent the night with and who has, unbeknown to him, fathered her baby son August. She explains that, eighteen months earlier, they had met in a bar and, in an attempt to explain the concept of hygge, she had taken him home. They ended up having sex but, when she woke in the morning, he had gone, leaving no name and no number. The resulting uproar was not caused by the many thousands of people who had been duped into believing that the film was real, or by feminists outraged by the stereotype, or even by pushers of family values shocked at the woman's loose morals. No; the real problem was that Danes felt it had misrepresented the true spirit of hygge. The reaction confirms my suspicion that while quiet, mutually appreciative unions with plenty of time for post-coital conversation might be hyggelig, hot, noisy, lust-driven couplings, all sensual euphoria and immodest pleasure, most certainly are not.

But back to my day. Once we finally surfaced, I had a long shower and made us a breakfast of scrambled eggs, coffee and toast, which we ate outside in the sunshine. The first proper outdoor breakfast of the year. An event to be cherished. The boyfriend then went off to do his Sunday things, leaving me alone. This was a test. It is one thing to while away a sunshiny Sunday with your lover; quite another, for me at least, to do it alone. All those uninterrupted hours could be used for work, or gardening, or finally painting the internal doors. But I had made a decision to hygge myself, and hygge myself I would. So I read. First the papers and then my book, *Crossing to Safety* by Wallace Stegner, in a sunny yellow cover as beautiful as the prose it contains.

I stopped to make myself lunch and then dozed on the unmown grass. I telephoned my gone-away son and my brother for no purpose other than to catch up, and then a friend called me for the same reason. I did not weed the herb patch or dust the bookshelves while we spoke; I simply sat in the sun and chatted as if they were there in the garden with me.

By the time I sat down for supper that evening, I felt not only rested but slightly euphoric. I had befriended Stegner's cast of characters in a way that is only possible if you read with total immersion rather than fighting through eyelids heavy with a day's worth of tiredness and I had given proper, considered attention to people I love. Judged in terms of quantifiable tasks completed, I had accomplished little. The comfrey and creeping buttercup still rioted unchecked through my flower beds; the dust still clumped in the corners of the house; my internal doors were still mouse brown and emails remained unopened. But those are mundanities in the scheme of things. A day spent weeding and dusting and emailing disappears; it is lost and wasted in the noise of daily living. But this day had not been wasted. This day had contributed to my stock of happiness.

$$\wedge\vee\wedge$$

The Monday after my hygge Sunday I was out running before seven (without so much as a goodbye to the sleeping boyfriend), and then put in a nine-hour stint in my hut. But the experience of the previous day had had a profound effect. It sounds ridiculous; all I had done was take a day off – and a Sunday at that – but thinking about it with a hygge mindset really had made a difference. The deal I had made with myself at the start of the day to run further and work harder than usual on the morrow was off by evening because I had realised that I did not need to make recompense. Monday's industry was not an act of penitence, therefore, but rather the result of a fresh mind and rested muscles.

A few years ago, in a column for the *Guardian* newspaper, the writer Oliver Burkeman speculated that the fact that the Danes had a word for the elusive sense of contentment that is so crucial to our well-being was a reason for their much-reported happiness. 'If you don't have a readily accessible label for a feeling such as hygge,' he wrote, 'might that not help edge it out of your emotional range, or at least from the kinds of things you find time in your schedule to do?'[10]

Burkeman is on to something. By naming hygge, the Danes have turned contentment, well-being, happiness, call it what you will (see the problem for those of us who do not have a word for it?), into a thing that they can do. And that is what is so distinctive about hygge. We all, whatever our nationalities, have days, or parts of days, when we stop. In the UK we might call it 'a pyjama day' on which we 'slob out' and 'do nothing'. But the language is both passive and negative. A pyjama day suggests slothful inactivity; the dictionary defines a slob as a lazy person with low standards of cleanliness; doing nothing implies that you are wasting your time. Had I thought of my Sunday in any of those terms, I would not have felt rested and euphoric by the evening, I would have felt rested and guilty. I am aware that my work ethic is overdeveloped, that my compulsion to achieve something each and every day is a kind of neurosis, but I don't believe I am the only one who feels that a day doing nothing is a wasted one and therefore something to be avoided. The Danes, on the other hand, do not do nothing, they 'hygge'. It is a verb. A doing word. An activity in itself.

A couple of the very many surveys I came across while I was working on this book cast an interesting light on the effect of consciously recognising downtime – particularly as I had just discovered that, according to Action for Happiness' Happiness Facts, 40 per cent of our potential for happiness is accounted for by our daily activities and the conscious choices we make. The International Social Survey Programme 2012 asked a selection of adults aged over eighteen to consider their lives in general and to say how happy they were on the whole.[11] 'Very', 'fairly' and 'completely' were grouped together for reasons that were not explained as far as I could tell. Denmark, unusually, did not make it into the top three (the podium places went to Iceland, Switzerland and the US). However, the 2011–12 European Quality of Life Survey asked adults, this time aged sixteen and over, a slightly different question; rather than asking if they felt their lives were happy, it asked whether they felt they were worthwhile.[12] Denmark came top in this survey (91.4 per cent of those questioned agreed, or strongly agreed, that what they did was worthwhile). I am speculating here, but might the Danes' belief that their lives have purpose have something to do with the fact that hygge recognises the validity of activities the rest of us might dismiss as inconsequential? A Brit would say that they had done nothing if they'd spent the evening curled up on the sofa in front of *The Bridge*. A Dane would say they had had themselves some hygge time.

The Danes don't hygge all the time; even they have to go to work, clean the house (they are a house-proud nation, and the etymological roots of hygge connect the word to notions of a well-kept, clean home) and get to the supermarket before closing time. 'We don't live entirely hyggelige lives,' The Happiness Research Institute's Meik Wiking told me, 'but we do make time for hygge moments when we can take a break from the demands and disciplines of everyday life.' Heidi Boye echoes his words in her thesis on hygge. 'Relaxation from a busy schedule is a fundamental part of hygge,' she writes. 'Hygge is the place where individuals' batteries are recharged.'[13]

Having given it a try, I became a convert to the self-hygging cause. I will never spend a day in my pyjamas. I do not own, and have no intention of buying, any 'super-comfy loungewear for chillin' out days' [sic], as one online clothing store put it, but I have started to pay proper attention to my downtime. I am learning to think that a Sunday morning spent reading the papers is time well spent, and therefore does not have to be atoned for with an afternoon of admin or gardening. I am teaching myself to believe that it is as good for me to stay talking in bed with my boyfriend on a Monday morning as it is to get up at 6.45 a.m. and go for a run. (He goes further, claiming that talking in bed is better than running, but then he is a GP and has seen his fill of middle-aged runners with permanently damaged knees.) The difference is subtle. I do not spend any more time hygging myself than I did 'doing nothing'; I still do the admin and the gardening and the housework, and I still run on a knee-damagingly regular basis, but the nagging voice in my head that took the shine off these times by telling me I should be doing something more productive has been silenced, more or less. I have learned that raising the white flag means surrendering wholeheartedly to these moments of self-kindness. 'Learning to relax, without shame, without guilt, is one of the great arts and solaces of life,' writes Anthony Seldon in his book *Beyond Happiness*.[14] He is right.

∧∨∧

The Danes do feel guilt. Of course they do; they are human, after all, not some species apart – despite the mythology. However, guilt and hygge are polar opposites; each repels the other. Given hygge's ubiquity, that must have an impact on the Danes' approach to life in general. This is a hunch, and I have no hard evidence to back it up, but hygge has given the Danes permission to pursue their personal happiness not just in small ways – guilt-free cake-eating, unapologetic binges on box sets of Nordic Noir – but in the big stuff too.

Guilt, as I have said, is something I am prone to. I don't know why; I am not Catholic, or even religious. But I am a middle-class, white British woman raised in an era when such women were expected to have it all. Our mothers had fought for our equal rights and we were expected to show our gratitude by combining stimulating, independent careers with fulfilling domestic lives. By chairing meetings in Jimmy Choo shoes and making flapjacks for the school cake sale while simultaneously faxing New York. (This was the mid-1990s; email had not yet reached us.) Some women managed it; most did not. When I announced that I was pregnant and planning to work only two or three days a week, and from home at that, the news was greeted with a disappointed silence. I felt guilty at letting down the sisterhood. But when I dropped my three-month-old son off at the childminder's, I felt guilty about letting him down too. Leaking breasts were a physical confirmation of my neglect.

And because it comes so easily, when I did something that really was a cause for guilt it consumed me. I left my first husband because I wasn't happy, which, as reasons to break up a home, felt about as self-centred as it was possible to be. Years ago, my father had left my mother in order to pursue his own happiness and for a long time I had thought it insufficient cause, yet here I was repeating history. A less self-flagellating personality would blame it on dodgy genes. I worried about passing them on.

I got over myself eventually – through a combination of time, running, wine, friends and a bit of counselling – but the experience convinced me that guilt is nothing but destructive. If we do something to hurt someone else then we should rightly feel remorse, but wallowing in our guilt does no one any good. It's more indulgence than atonement.

What I had not fully come to terms with until I started looking into hygge was the validity of my reason for leaving. Hygge does not offer absolution. How could it? It is essentially just a concept advocating pleasant, and often convivial, contentedness as an antidote to the stresses of daily life. However, as I have already explored, it has given the Danes a real understanding of the importance of personal happiness.

As part of the empirical research for his paper 'Money Can't Buy Me Hygge', Jeppe Trolle Linnet sought out discourses on hygge on various websites. One he came across featured a group of Danes discussing attitudes to divorce, including the difficult issue of how hard parents should work at keeping the marriage together for the sake of the children. 'The prevailing notion,' Linnet writes, 'was that while one should indeed attempt to save the relationship, if it had deteriorated to the point where no hyggelig atmosphere could be found in the home, then a divorce was the only solution – not least for the children who should not grow up in cold, non-hyggelige surroundings.'[15]

This is fascinating. First, it implies that the Danes believe marriage should be a hyggelig state (which, if you think about the cornerstones of hygge – contentment, pleasant sociability and an atmosphere in which everyone feels safe and plays an equal part – is a very fine thing to believe) and second, that if one or both parties is not experiencing hygge, then it is reasonable that they should seek a divorce. Of course, breaking apart a shared life is devastating; it shatters the people involved. But marriages in which habit usurps love and spouses chip away at each other's happiness through neglect born of complacency, or with a million sharp-edged gibes, shatter people too. It just happens more slowly.

I am sure the Danes take divorce seriously; I am sure that most of them try to make things work and wrestle with the question of whether simply being unhappy is enough. But I also believe that the knock-on effects of hygge help more of them to accept that it is. It's easy to sneer at the Danes' high divorce rate, to take it as evidence of an inability to make successful relationships, but you could look at it the other way round. Just as the high level of anti-depressant usage could indicate that they take severe unhappiness seriously, rather than suffer from higher than average rates of depression, so the divorce rate might be due to the fact that they regard marriage as something too important to do badly. It was the Danish philosopher Søren Kierkegaard who came up with the phrase 'better well hanged than ill wed'.

In 2008, the *British Medical Journal* published a report on research into the dynamic spread of happiness in a large social network. The research involved measuring the happiness of 4,739 individuals over the course of twenty years (1983–2003), with the aim of evaluating whether happiness can spread from person to person. The conclusion was that indeed it could. Apparently, people whose close contacts are happy have a 15 per cent greater chance of being happy themselves. The report's authors finish the summary with the unambiguous statement: 'People's happiness depends on the happiness of others with whom they are connected.'[16]

If happiness is contagious then it follows that we owe it to those closest to us to take our own happiness seriously. 'The pursuit of happiness . . . is anything but selfish,' writes Antony Seldon in *Beyond Happiness*. 'Relatives, friends and colleagues all benefit when we are happy. Their lives are diminished when we are unhappy. The pursuit of joy is a moral duty.'[17] Or to put it in Bobby McFerrin's more musical way, '. . . be happy, 'cause when you worry your face will frown and that will bring everybody down'.

# CELEBRATING THE SIMPLE

Hygge is an understated thing. Jeppe Trolle Linnet, rather wittily, called his article examining the social phenomenon of hygge 'Money Can't Buy Me Hygge', and should you play hygge word association with a Dane, the chances are that the words 'modest', 'simple' and 'low key' will crop up almost as frequently as 'cosy' and 'family'.

It is difficult for an outsider to grasp precisely what hygge simplicity means. After all, hyggelige homes seem to be furnished with plenty of stuff; and Hans Wegner's Wishbone chairs may be low key, but the price tags could hardly be described as modest. Like all deep-seated cultural practices, the nuances are instinctive to natives and a mere fog to everyone else, so I will let Linnet provide some illumination.

During his research, he interviewed an affluent middle-aged couple who believed that it was important to provide a hyggelig home for their three children. In one exchange Linnet documents, they are discussing household chores. The couple explain that the family do the housework together – no small feat, given their apartment measures 200 square metres. 'Why not get a cleaning lady to do it?' Linnet asks. 'We could, but no,' comes the response, 'it actually  becomes really hyggelig when we do it all together.' They move on to discuss holidays, and the couple are disparaging about families whose vacations involve flying ever greater distances in search of ever greater thrills. They plan to go to Berlin, and will stay in a 'sensible' hotel. 'It's no use staying in an eight-star Hilton,' the husband says, ' I like it to be a little bit hyggelig.'

Clearly for this couple hygge is the very opposite of excess. It is first and foremost about doing something ordinary, or at least unshowy, and doing it as a family. Linnet suggests that this couple's barely concealed disapproval of extravagance reflects an understanding of hygge that is common among the Danish middle classes. 'Hygge figures as a marker of "real" family togetherness,' he writes,

which is opposed to experiences that are either exotic and dramatic or luxurious and characterised by some degree of upscale formality. The realm of the exotic and luxurious is presented as 'overdoing it', as something that goes beyond what is necessary or 'enough' for enjoying close personal relations and, indeed, makes a hyggelig atmosphere less likely to arise. Thrift is a way not only to save money but also to remain at a level where things and relations are 'real', with hygge as a marker of this 'real-ness'.[18]

Before we head off down this ever so humble path towards some homespun, candlelit version of nirvana, I do need to say one thing: celebrating the simple is a privilege of the comfortably off. Choosing to eschew conspicuous consumption might bring pleasure, but having it thrust upon you certainly does not. Only the affluent are able to relish the modest joy of hanging out the laundry on a line in the sunshine; poor people are too busy worrying about how they will pay for the electricity to power the washing machine.

I am fortunate. I have never had to worry about where the next meal will come from, or whether an unexpected knock on the door is a bailiff come for his dues. However, shortly after moving to the bungalow, I lost a contract with a local arts organisation I had been working with. Contracts mean guaranteed money and are thus highly prized by freelancers. This was the only one I had and it paid the mortgage; without it, there was a possibility that in a slow month I could earn nothing at all. I sat down with my bank statements and bills and did some depressing sums. Clearly, horns would have to be drawn in until I found some more regular work.

I have always thought that I was happy to live modestly in my small house, with my small car and a natural preference for meeting friends over supper at home rather than out in fancy restaurants. However, when my temporary underemployment meant that I had no option but to have another quiet night in reading in the company of a slow-cooked rustic bean stew, I found that life grew dull. When modest is all there is it loses its appeal, and it is no coincidence that I made my decision to try and live a more hyggelig life once this frugal phase had come to an end.

Linnet's interviewees might have managed to turn the weekly house clean into a moment of family hygge, but I knew that was beyond me. (I blame this particular domestic failing on the fact that I am not Danish.) What I was interested in was the idea that, rather than adopting a whole new set of hyggelige activities, I could simply hyggefy the ones which already filled my days. I began with breakfast.

I have always liked breakfast; the food is heavy on the carbs (always a good thing in my opinion), predictable (thus eliminating any need to think about what you might eat), easy to prepare and, as I have usually been out for a run beforehand, necessary from a calorific point of view. Muesli is ambrosial when you're hungry. But I tend to eat it standing at the kitchen worktop as I go through my emails, which means that the meal only registers as fuel. One morning I was standing over my laptop, my mouth full of muesli, reading an email from one of my Danish correspondents. She was describing how she tried to make every meal a little hygge moment by laying the table and lighting a candle. It sounded such a lovely idea, and so easy – I have a scrubbed wooden table and an extensive collection of hand-thrown crockery in a range of chalky colours to put on it. I have several giant bags of those IKEA tea lights stuffed in the cupboard under the kitchen sink. Getting to the office involves nothing more than walking across the deck to my hut and, since no one knows whether I am at the kitchen table or at my desk anyway, it doesn't matter if breakfast takes a little longer.

The next morning I took time to choose crockery in pleasing, toning shades. It was a faded-out day, the wood and the sky above it made pale by the early-morning mist, so I went for a hint-of-grey mug, a hint-of-blue bowl and a plate the colour of a wisp of smoke. I put them all on the wooden table and stood back to admire my tableau. I did think about a candle, but it was Tuesday morning, I was all alone and this is Gloucestershire, not Copenhagen. I made coffee, savouring the smell and sound of my tarnished, grain-ingrained Moka Express coming to the boil on the stove. I sat down. That first morning I did log into my email account, but even with that distraction, this breakfast felt different; a brief moment of pleasure on an ordinary working morning.

Since then I have made some other minor changes. I have started having a bath instead of a shower on a Sunday morning after the club run, pouring it hot and deep and soaking until my skin wrinkles. If I am all alone, I put some music on and sing along to vintage pop as I lie up to my neck in bubbles (T. Rex's 'Cosmic Dancer' is a particular favourite). I now set the alarm half an hour early on the occasional morning to give me time to lie in bed and read before I get up, a treat previously reserved solely for holidays. I have started listening to podcasts of radio plays while I do the ironing and I am amazed – and slightly embarrassed – to admit that this has turned a chore into something really rather hyggelig. And when weather and workload permit, I have taken to drinking my late-afternoon cup of tea on the bench outside. These are the smallest and simplest of pleasures, but I enjoy each individual one, and a week in which I have made time to indulge in several of them is a very contented week indeed. A hyggelig week.

# FOCUSING ON THE MOMENT

Hygge must not be rushed. In the English summary of her paper, Heidi Boye observes that 'time is important for the constitution of hygge'.[19] She is talking about quality rather than quantity. A hyggelig moment need last no more than a few minutes, so long as those minutes receive the undivided attention of everyone involved. As the members of her focus group explain, to be hyggelig 'time [must not] flow together with other chores. It is qualitatively different and exists as a space where the hygge activity unfolds'.

We live in an age when everything, from communication to dating, is getting faster. According to Robert Colvile's book *The Great Acceleration: How the World is Getting Faster, Faster*, we are now even walking more quickly than our parents and grandparents did.[20] And as we walk, we also talk on the phone, send instant messages, surf the web. Multitasking is clever – humans are the only species that can do it – but it's not very good for us, apparently.

In 2010, Daniel T. Gilbert, a professor of psychology at Harvard, and doctoral psychology student Matthew A. Killingsworth unveiled the details of their investigation into whether a wandering mind is also an unhappy one. They had developed an app which contacted adults through their iPhones at random moments during the day and presented them with questions about their happiness and mind-wandering. Their answers were recorded on a database. Gilbert and Killingsworth then analysed samples from 2,250 of the participants and discovered that mind-wandering occurred in 46.9 per cent of the sample in every activity they engaged in other than sex. More disturbingly, it showed that participants were significantly less happy when their minds wandered than they were when they were still. In the report of their findings, the pair concluded that 'a wandering mind is an unhappy mind. The ability to think about what is not happening is a cognitive achievement that comes at an emotional cost.' [21]

The Vietnamese Buddist monk Thích Nhất Hạnh didn't need an app to tell him that. Hạnh is revered around the world for his teaching and writings on mindfulness. 'The present moment is filled with joy and happiness,' he advises. 'If you are attentive, you will see it.' Mindfulness has become the twenty-first century's most fashionable route to well-being. Celebrities do it; companies from Google to the British Home Office and the US military do it; and on 20 October 2015, a cross-party group of British politicians launched a programme called Mindful Nation UK, recommending that mindfulness training be introduced into schools, the NHS and the criminal justice system.

Defined as 'bringing attention to the present moment on purpose and without judgement', mindfulness is an ancient practice derived from Buddhism and is fundamental to many of the world's religions. Contemporary Western mindfulness is the creation of Jon Kabat-Zinn, who founded the Stress Reduction Clinic at the University of Massachusetts Medical School in the late 1970s. His Mindfulness Based Stress Reduction programme (MBSR) aims to help with conditions as diverse as chronic pain, heart disease, psoriasis, sleep problems and depression and, to date, more than eighteen thousand people have completed the course. A variation on his technique, Mindfulness Based Cognitive Therapy (MBCT) was developed in the 1990s and has been approved in the UK as the 'treatment of choice for depression' by the National Institute for Clinical Excellence.

I do not doubt the efficacy of either MBSR or MBCT. I am a great believer in using talking therapies rather than pills to treat depression and anxiety. When I had a panic attack so severe that I almost drove into a lorry on the M4 motorway, I signed up for several months of talk-based counselling, and I am eternally grateful to my doctor for not even suggesting that I take a load of tablets instead. But I am now cured of my panic attacks; I am not depressed; I do not suffer from psoriasis and I sleep the sleep of a dead person (other than when the premenopausal night sweats strike, and I'm not sure mindfulness is a cure for that), so I am resistant to the idea of going on one of the ever-burgeoning mindfulness courses. It is my failing, I am sure, but I have always been irritated by the spiritual pyschobabble of people who call themselves 'life coaches', and the self-help end of the mindfulness industry seems to attract them in droves. I do not want to 'anchor my awareness'; the tautology implicit in an instruction to 'shut my eyes and watch my body breathing' infuriates me and I have no idea how to 'ride the waves of my breath'. If it's anything like surfing, it will end in a nastily twisted ankle.

However, the idea which lies at the heart of mindfulness, that we would all be happier if we focused on the moment, is an echo of hygge's requirement for mental presence. Deep down, I probably knew that it was better to focus on the present moment rather than constantly wonder what will follow it long before I came across hygge, but I didn't give it a try due to my aversion to all things self-help. Discovering that mental presence could be achieved without having to learn any special techniques was transformative. Even I could embrace an idea that simply means making an effort not to multitask from time to time. Call it 'Mindfulness Lite', if you like, but it works for me. (I wondered whether it worked for the Danes, too; whether their habitual practice of hygge meant that they didn't need mindfulness, but a quick online search for courses suggested not. It seems that mindfulness is as much of a thing in Denmark as it is in the UK.)

I am an inveterate multitasker, so it hasn't been easy. I am focused when I'm working; shut away in my hut, I am frequently surprised by the arrival of the postman, but in the rest of my life, I have always worked on the principle that the more things you can combine the better. I cook with the telephone wedged under my ear, I eat over my laptop and I clean the bathroom basin at the same time as my teeth. My phone is rarely out of my sight, and I am quick to jump to its bidding. But I have now made some changes. I leave my mobile at home when I go for a walk; if I call a friend then I sit down in a comfortable chair and concentrate on our conversation (it doesn't always work if they call me – I find it difficult to be in the moment when I am caught off guard). One morning a week I turn my computer off while I eat my breakfast, and I have plans to do the same on the occasional lunch break. I have also reassessed how I run.

In 'Food and Health in Late Modernity: An Insight into Hygge and Related Food Practices', Heidi Boye documents conversations she had with a Danish focus group about their understanding of hygge. When it came to discussing participation in sport, they were split: the fitness fans believed that exercise could be hyggelig (one woman even described running in silent step with her husband as one of the most hyggelig things she did), while those who led more sedentary lives did not. What they were all agreed on was that sweat, excessive breathlessness and competition killed off hygge as effectively as a family row.

This discovery was important. I am a woman who runs, and when I embarked on this hygge experiment I just assumed that running would qualify since I set time aside to do it and it made me feel relaxed. It never occurred to me that running in the way I do might not be hyggelig at all. Clearly I could hardly claim to be fully embracing the hygge philosophy if I spent so much of my leisure time doing something it excluded; if I was to continue, then I had to start running in a more hyggelig way. Less pushing myself into sweaty, breathless personal bests with the help of high-tech timers, and more running simply for the sake of running. I wasn't sure I could do it, particularly as one of the reasons I started running in the first place was that it provided an outlet for my competitive streak.

Life as a home-based freelance writer with an instinctive aversion to adult team sports doesn't provide much opportunity for competition. A fact which explains why I found myself storming the mother's race one primary school summer. I hadn't intended to win. As I lined up with the other barefoot mums, skirts discreetly tucked into our knicker legs, it didn't occur to me that anyone would come first. But when the starter bell rang, I set off at a sprint and won by an embarrassing margin. I'd like to say that I was simply faster than the others, but the photos show the truth; eyes straight, jaw set, I ran that race to win. And, deep down, I was proud.

Several years later, the man who was to become my second ex-husband announced that he was going for a jog. This wasn't unusual; he ran most weeks to balance a working life rich in Mayfair lunches, but this time the crisp air of a London spring seemed tempting and I was curious. I hadn't been for a run since the sixth form, when weekly cross-country treks were compulsory (we soon found that all routes led to a copse dense enough to hide several smokers), but as a pre-teen I had run for the school. I found a pair of old Green Flash trainers in the cupboard and off we set through the suburban streets of south-west London towards the Thames.

We were still in step by the time we reached the towpath a mile or so later. I was feeling rather puffed, truth be told, but the thought that I could beat him, this man who beat me so thoroughly at everything else, was glucose. I sped up, the slightly too-small Green Flash chafing my little toes, and reached the bridge before he did. Ex number two hadn't realised that this friendly Saturday-morning jog was really a race, but so what? I had won and I was triumphant; my blood flowed, my muscles sang. Before I could stop myself, I had punched the air.

We never ran together again, but I was off. Here was a sport that I could do without joining a team and which allowed me to compete whenever I went out. All I needed was a route planner so that I could measure my distances and a path popular with other runners, all of whom I regarded as targets to be passed. I gave chase to anyone in front of me and was incapable of letting someone overtake without forcing them to race me first. On one occasion, hearing nearing footsteps, I sped up and my anonymous competitor and I sprinted the two miles from Barnes railway bridge to Hammersmith before I finally gave in.

I began to sign up for races. Half-marathons and then, inevitably, a marathon. Half-marathons are about competing against other people; marathons, for me at least, are all about competing against yourself. There is a school of thought that says the human body is designed to run a maximum of 22 miles. A marathon is 26.2. The reason I wanted to run one was to see whether I could beat my body by pushing it those extra four or so miles. And it turned out that I could, so I did it again, faster.

Then my second marriage ended, and running became the only way I could find to stop the noise. The morning after the big reveal, I woke up alone and, not knowing what else to do, I went for a run. It was August and I was in Dorset so I set off up the Downs with their close-cropped grass, on up the shady trail that follows the cliff edge of Durlston Bay, past the super-sized Victorian stone globe with its carved colonial map, down the stony path above the open sea, fleetingly keeping pace with a fishing boat motoring far below; around the lighthouse, long given over to holiday lets but on this morning at least still appearing to flash its warning as the sun hit its windows. Up and up to the very top of the cliff edge and, finally, out onto the open meadows. Running quick and sure across the clifftop, my mind stilled until I was nothing but blood and breath and muscle. I knew that I could stop the truth being true as long as I kept running, so I did. Until thirst made me realise that I'd been out for two hours and that, at some point, I would have to go home.

I ran like that for the next twelve months. Ever-increasing miles along Gloucestershire's lanes, out on the high commons and through the shedding and then budding woods; to keep me sane, off the bottle and exhausted enough to sleep at night. It was manic and bad for my back, but as a coping mechanism it worked. It also made me so fit that I started picking up the odd medal.

And that's where I was when I read that focus group's thoughts about hygge and exercise: overexerted, highly competitive and more focused on the result of the activity than the activity itself. But I really wanted to do this hygge thing, and so, helped by an injury that left me physically unable to do anything more than jog gently along a flat lane at the bottom of the valley for several weeks, I pulled out of the London Marathon, took off my watch, deactivated my MapMyRun account and stopped doing efforts with the club.

Running with no purpose beyond pleasure is slightly less easy to do than say, but I am getting there. Leaving behind my timing devices means that I have become acutely aware of how I feel, and I have tuned into the sound of my breath, the rhythm of my feet. Not caring how far or how fast I go means that I run with a child's delight in the possibility of my limbs – albeit slightly marred by the inevitable niggles of a middle-aged runner who has run too much.

Running like this gives me a very precise sense of place. I don't notice the particularities of the landscape in the same way as I do when I'm walking, but I have become acutely aware of the terrain and the seasons.

Spring is bluebells and wood anemones and the acrid edge of wild garlic on the breeze. High summer is brown at the edges; dusty and slightly wilted, and I run early to make the most of the still-fresh sun. Autumn is the month of damp seven o'clock lanes when the mist fades the landscape, the leaves mulch under my feet and the air forms droplets on my eyelashes. In autumn I head for the woods where I can breathe the wet, loamy earth and watch the pale sun stripe through the beech trees. I don't do patriotism, but I was born in the English countryside in a landscape of woods and valleys where the fog can hang all day, so misle, that misty drizzle that Gloucestershire does so well, is in my bones. The dampness of an English autumn roots me. And winter is cold. Nothing beats the exhilaration of running over frozen fields, the air sharp in your throat, the wind bringing tears to your eyes, and when the sun shines on the frosty dogwoods, I know that all is right with the world. Of course, more often than not, winter just means rain, which makes it hard to leave the house, but it's fun once I'm out. Splashing through the puddles makes me laugh.

For me, running has always been a good way of finding some silence, but this new, hygge-inspired running has taken the silence to another level. Now that I don't even think about the distance I have travelled or the speed I have gone or the calories I have used, my head is empty. I'd be lying if I said I never thought about racing or that I had completely stopped making shopping lists in my head as I go, but more often than not these days I am just out in the air and running.

Positive Psychologists would describe this state as 'flow'; the Danes would most likely concede that it was hyggelig, despite the sweat and occasional breathlessness. In Positive Psychology, flow is just one stage on the journey towards a flourishing state of well-being. In hygge, there is no journey. Simply taking some time out to let your soul catch up with your body is enough.

'*The Danes have a shared unconscious idea about what hygge is (and what it isn't), which transcends all aspects of public and private life. It often manifests itself in food and drink. Being aware of your surroundings and feeling comfortable is important, too. Taking an interest in the home and making an effort to create a nice space has always been essential to me, and consequently I've spent a lot of time trying to transform our old, draughty, single-glazed Victorian house into something warm and inviting*'

# HOW TO HYGGE:
## SOUL

# HYGGE YOURSELF HAPPY

Hygge is not the secret of personal happiness. And nor is the Danes' widespread hygge habit the only reason that they are consistently ranked as one of the world's happiest nations. But while hygge may not be a miracle cure for discontent (and no Danish person I have spoken to has ever made that claim), my research into the concept has convinced me that its practice does have a positive impact on the daily lives of the citizens of Denmark, and could therefore have something to offer the rest of us.

This book is my personal exploration of hygge, and one which I have deliberately conducted from a foreign shore, so what follows here is simply a compilation of the hygge-inspired things that I have introduced into my life and which I feel have added to my store of happiness. I make no claim for their authenticity in Danish terms, and I can't promise that they will make any difference to your sense of well-being, but since most of them require nothing more than a few small, pleasurable adjustments to a daily routine and a slight shift in thinking, there is little to be lost in giving the ideas a try. What I can promise is that nothing here involves decluttering, detoxing or following any sort of course.

## Give yourself a break

Meik Wiking, CEO of The Happiness Research Institute, describes hyggelige times as moments when Danish people 'raise the white flag and take a break from the demands and disciplines of everyday life'. One of the Danes I spoke to about their personal understanding of hygge told me that she felt it was about 'making time to let your soul catch up with your body'. These statements get to the heart of what I find most appealing about hygge. The philosophy behind it is that we should all practise self-kindness and learn to cherish ourselves a little more, which we should, but put like that it sounds rather abstract. How exactly do we go about cherishing ourselves? Translated from therapy-speak into the straightforward language of hygge, the idea is easy to grasp. It just means having regular time out in which we do something gentle and pleasant without feeling guilty about it. And that sounds very achievable indeed. Here are six suggestions:

1   **Turn functional meals into an event.** I am not suggesting that you transform your weekday breakfasts and working lunches into culinary extravaganzas (although do go ahead if you wish), but just because we often eat breakfast and lunch alone and at speed, doesn't mean that we can't savour them. Instead of standing at the kitchen worktop, I now sit down to eat my breakfast every morning, taking time to choose crockery that looks and feels good, and, once a week, I also make an effort to put my phone away and leave my laptop unopened so that I can concentrate fully on the smell and taste of the food. I do the same at lunchtime. It goes without saying that all this is a great deal easier if you work at home, but you can hyggefy office meals too. Ditch the cracked cup and snack-bar packaging and keep a favourite

plate and mug in the work kitchen. Find somewhere to eat that is away from your desk, or at least clear a space and switch your computer to sleep mode. The meal might be nothing more than a shop-bought sandwich, and it may only take ten minutes to consume, but you can turn those ten minutes into a small moment of peaceable pleasure in a working day.

2   **Go for a walk.** Because I don't commute, I do this at the end of my writing day before I tackle the emails and admin, but a walk could be your journey to the bus stop in the morning, or a turn around the block in your lunch break. It's not about exercise; it is about taking half an hour to notice the land- or townscape and, if you go with someone else, to enjoy their company. Leave your phone behind and don't count your steps.

3   **Wake up early and read before you get up.** Reading in bed in the morning is one of my greatest holiday pleasures, but as I don't go on holiday all that often, I decided to try and incorporate this treat into my day-to-day life by setting the alarm half an hour early. I don't do it every morning, but when I do, I always get out of bed feeling that I have had a rather indulgent lie-in. (It has made a significant difference to my consumption of contemporary fiction, too.) You don't have to read – you could listen to the radio, talk to your partner, have a cup of tea, make love – the point is to enjoy some time in bed awake before you get up and face the day.

4   **Pour yourself a glass of wine and phone a friend.** Pre-hygge, I always multitasked while I was on the telephone – just sitting and chatting seemed a waste of time when I could clamp the receiver under my ear and get on with some boring domestic chore. I am not completely rehabilitated, but these days I am

doing less housework and more drinking and chatting. Especially if the weather is warm enough for me to sit on the bench in the garden. Concentrating solely on the conversation makes me feel that my friend and I have actually spent some time together.

5  **Have a bath.** Showers are brilliant at getting you clean and waking you up, but if you want a relaxing sensory experience, nothing beats a bath. I had never had a bath in the bungalow until I began this hygge thing, but I now spend an hour soaking in the tub most Sundays. Sometimes I read, and when I am alone in the house, I put the music on loud and sing along to my favourite tunes. And sometimes I just lie up to my ears in sweet-smelling foam and listen to the bubbles pop.

6  **Hyggefy a regular task.** Most of us have more things to do in a day than there are hours in which to do them, so, rather than adding to all the busyness with new hyggelige things, try hyggefying something you already do. I have started listening to podcasts of radio plays while I do the ironing, a chore that is now proving so enjoyable I have started ironing my sheets for the first time in my life. And I have discovered that getting into freshly ironed sheets is a pleasure to be savoured. Result? Double hygge.

## Notice your downtime

When I started talking about hygge, lots of my friends said it just sounded like a trendy, Scandi term for slobbing out. They were wrong. The activities may be similar – staying in your pyjamas on the sofa all day, for example – but the mindsets are completely different. If we spend a day slobbing out, we dismiss it as a day spent 'doing nothing', which means that at best we consider it of no importance and at worst we feel guilty about such wasted time. Hygging yourself, by contrast, is a conscious activity that is named, recognised and enjoyed for what it is. Not only does that mean there's no guilt to taint the pleasure, it also means that you are fully aware of the good this temporary retreat from the world is doing.

There are crossovers with mindfulness here. Mindfulness urges us to be fully present; hygge stipulates that for something to be truly hyggelig, the person or people involved must be fully engaged in the activity, however inactive that activity is. If you are reading, go somewhere quiet and devote yourself to your reading; if you are sitting with a glass of wine in front of the fire, concentrate on the taste of the wine and the flicker of the flames; if you are walking in the woods, notice the smell of the earth, the colours of the leaves, the patina of moss on bark; if you are out in a bar talking to a friend, focus on nothing but your conversation and listen as much as you speak. There are no meditation techniques to learn with hygge, but this total immersion in the moment does require some conscious effort. I have found that the secret is to tell myself that when I am curled on the sofa with the weekend papers, or lying in the sunny garden simply staring at the sky, I am not doing nothing. I am hygging myself, and that is important.

And because it is important, you need to make it part of your weekly routine. Schedule that hour in bed doing the crossword, or that lunch break in the local park with a friend into your weekly timetable. That time is as vital to your overall sense of well-being as a spin class – and a great deal more important than the housework.

## Celebrate the simple

Hygge is not about the high life. That doesn't mean you have to eschew all things hedonistic, it just means that you can't count a night of champagne-fuelled feasting and dancing as one of your weekly hyggelige moments. Which is good, as, for most of us, life offers more opportunities to celebrate simplicity than to indulge in excess.

Here are ten ideas:

1   **Make your morning coffee in a stovetop pot.** Don't do anything while it comes to the boil other than listen to the sound of the steam and breathe in that coffee-scented air.

2   **And drink it in a mug that looks and feels good.** Whether your taste is for hand-thrown and slightly wobbly stoneware, delicate fine bone china or a pint pot with your name on, drinking from a mug that pleases you aesthetically will enhance the experience no end.

3   **Pick your own.** Inheriting a vegetable patch was a surprise joy of moving to the bungalow. I loathe digging and mowing the lawn, so I had never been a big fan of gardening, but I have discovered that picking vegetables that I have grown myself brings a primal pleasure. I stick to the easy stuff – herbs, those pick-and-grow-again salad leaves, chard, rocket (all of which could be grown in a window box or pot outside the front door), because I don't think there is anything very hyggelig about spending the weekends training things up canes. For me, it is all about gathering produce still warm from the sun and turning it into a salad to feed my friends. And watering; there's nothing quite like the smell of cool water on hot soil.

4   **Peg the washing out on a real line.** It is not everyone's idea of a hyggelig moment, I'm sure, but to me, hanging the washing in the garden and watching it flap in the breeze means that summer has come and the boys are home. Old-fashioned wooden dolly pegs add a finishing touch.

5   **Embrace the weather.** The Danes are good at this. In summer they picnic and barbecue in the many public parks to make the most of the warm days and long, light evenings, but even in the winter you see them cycling through the rain and the snow and sitting wrapped in blankets outside cafés. They have a saying: 'There's no such thing as bad weather, just the wrong sort of clothes', and it's true. So what if it's freezing? Wrap yourself in an oversized sweater and go for a walk in the crunchy grass. Raining again? Put on your wellingtons and find a puddle to jump in. Come summer, head for the garden, the park, the beach or a town bench and spend half an hour just soaking up the sunshine.

6   **Have a picnic.** Eating sandwiches on the grass is a very fine thing indeed. Do it alone with a book or add wine and your favourite people. And why wait for summer? Picnics in the rain might be miserable, but a picnic in an autumn wood, all crisp leaves and russet colours, is an event to be savoured.

7   **Light a fire.** Or, if that's not possible, you can create a similar effect with a mass of candles. Put them on the floor (standing on something fireproof like a tile) and pull some comfy chairs around them.

8   **Bake something.** The pleasures of baking are many and various. Beating and stirring are gentle activities requiring just enough concentration to keep your mind from wandering; the smells are glorious and fill the house with both comfort and promise and the end result is deliciously satisfying. You don't need to make anything fancy; flapjacks will do, and if you want to be a little bit Danish, buy yourself a Margrethe mixing bowl. Invented in the 1950s, and named after Queen Margrethe II of Denmark, these melamine bowls are a design classic. They come in a range of lovely colours, too.

9   **Fill a jug with flowers.** If you can pick them yourself, do (creeping buttercups might be a nuisance in your flower beds, but they are joyous on the kitchen table), otherwise choose seasonal blooms with a heady scent.

10  **Give yourself a sensory treat.** A daily dose of sensory pleasure can only make you feel good. Cook your favourite food; run a bath filled with deliciously perfumed oils; pour yourself a glass of your favourite wine; light a scented candle; wrap yourself in a soft woollen throw. Sensory overload is not hygge, so focus on one sense at a time and give yourself over to the pleasure of the moment.

*'Hygge brings people together and filters through most aspects of daily life, which makes it rather difficult to pinpoint a specific moment that encapsulates it. However, living abroad away from friends and family means that I now associate Skype with hygge; for example "knitting nights" with my two best friends from back home, where we chat while doing various bits of handicraft and drinking the odd glass of wine, just like we did when we were younger and lived nearer each other. There's nothing mystical or unobtainable in it at all, but it is definitely hyggelig'*

# AFTERWORD

I read somewhere that one of the highest compliments one Dane can pay another is to describe him or her as 'man hviler sig selv'; someone who rests in him- or herself. It means being happy in your own skin, but I like the idea of people 'resting' in themselves. The profound sense of relaxation it implies seems to me to be an evocative summation of the spirit of hygge, and it is entirely fitting that a country with hygge at its heart should rate resting in yourself so highly.

I don't think anyone who has met me more than once would describe me in quite those terms, but this hygge experiment has, I believe, got me closer to resting in myself than I have been since the untroubled days of early childhood. I am certainly much better at allowing myself to enjoy time out – giving downtime a name really does make a difference to those of us who need always to feel that we are doing something.

I have not stopped multitasking, but I do it less and that has not only meant I enjoy the walk, the telephone call or the solitary cup of coffee more than I did in the past, it has lowered my stress levels too. I have found that the disquieting sense that I am a poorly trained juggler on the verge of dropping all of her balls disappears when I focus on one thing at a time.

And I have learned that, sometimes, avoiding confrontation and prioritising harmony is the right, rather than the lazy, approach to family life.

Am I happier as a result? Today, a sunny Thursday late in May 2016, I am certainly happier than I have been in a long time, although I suspect much is owed to the healing passing of time as it is to hygge. What I am sure of, though, is that daily life is a great deal nicer now that it is punctuated by regular hygge moments.

At school if you described something as 'nice', the English teacher would cross it out and tell you to find a more emphatic word – 'wonderful', 'beautiful', 'amazing'. But having an amazing time is quite different to having a nice time. It's hedonia versus eudaimonia all over again. Amazing is high-octane and heart-quickening, whereas nice is low key and gentle. It cocoons you. So when I say life is nicer, that's what I mean. Introducing hygge into my life has made it more cocooning. And that is not to be sneered at.

Of course, too much cocooning could be suffocating, and there is a certain interiority to hygge that is troubling. It is a concept that looks in rather than out, that puts comfort and security at its centre; that advocates huddling around the home fire with family and close friends while strangers and storms rage outside. The ease of hygge is seductive, and it would be easy to overdo things, easy to lapse into the kind of self-satisfied withdrawal from the challenges of life that I have always resisted.

But then to overdo hygge would be most unhyggelig. Everything in moderation is the hygge way, even hygge itself. As mottoes go, I accept that it lacks excitement – it's hardly 'carpe diem', after all – but for a woman with a tendency to seize things and not let them go, it is a message worth remembering. Faced with the dying of the light, I would still choose to rage, but this experiment with hygge has shown me that, sometimes, there is a lot to be said for going gently.

*'Hygge is part of the Danish culture as we have very long, very dark winters with miserable weather. If you have no one to share the time with then you may find that the winter becomes very long and depressing. You need these small events in your life which you plan in detail and surprise your family or friends with. Hygge is an integrated part of our lives; we would not live without hygge'*

# A WORD ON THE GRAMMAR

**Hygge** (hoo-ga) noun; verb

**Hyggelig**; **hyggeligt** – adjective, singular

The spelling follows the gender of the noun. Danish nouns are divided into common or neuter rather than masculine and feminine; hyggelig is used with common nouns (e.g. en hyggelig dag – a cosy day) and hyggeligt with neuter nouns (e.g. et hyggeligt hus – a common house). As English nouns have no gender, I have opted to use hyggelig throughout this book.

**Hyggelige** – adjective, plural regardless of gender

With apologies to the Danes, I have also invented a couple of variations – hygging, which I use as a Gerund (e.g. 'I am hygging myself'), and hyggefy, by which I mean to make something hyggelig.

# WHERE TO BUY

## Carl Hansen & Søn

Bredgade 18, 21 and 23,
1260 Copenhagen K,
Denmark

+45 6447 2360

and

16a Bowling Green Lane,
London  EC1R OBD

+44 (0)20 7632 7587

www.carlhansen.com

## Design by Dane

+ 45 20 83 63 94
www.designbydane.com

## dk3

Spinderigade 11, 7100 Vejle,
Denmark

+45 70 70 21 70
www.dk3.dk

and

TwentyTwentyOne,
274–5 Upper Street,
London  N1 2UA

+44 020 7288 1996
www.twentytwentyone.com

## Fredericia

Frederiksborggade 22,
DK-1360 Copenhagen K

+45 3312 4644
www.fredericia.com

and

TwentyTwentyOne,
274–5 Upper Street,
London  N1 2UA

+44 (0)20 7288 1996
www.twentytwentyone.com

## Fritz Hansen

Vestergaard Møbler,
Torvegade 55–57,
1400 Copenhagen K

+45 3257 2814
www.vester-moebler.dk

and

Republic of Fritz Hansen,
13 Margaret Street,
London  W1W 8RN

+44 (0)7637 5534
www.fritzhansen.com

## Hay

Hay House, Oestergade 61,
2nd and 3rd Floor,
1100 Copenhagen, Denmark

+45 42 820 820
www.hay.dk

and

Nest

+44 (0)114 243 3000
www.nest.co.uk

## Le Klint

Store Kirkestræde 1,
DK-1073 Copenhagen K,
Denmark

+45 3311 6663
www.leklint.com

and

Skandium,
245–9 Brompton Road,
London  SW3 2EP

+44 020 7584 2066
www.skandium.com

## Louis Poulsen

A/S Gammel Strand 28,
DK-1202 Copenhagen, Denmark

+45 7033 1414
www.louispoulsen.com

and

Viaduct,
1–10 Summers Street,
London  EC1R 5BD

+44 (0)20 7278 8456
www.viaduct.co.uk

## Normann Copenhagen

Normann Copenhagen,
Østerbrogade 70,
2100 Copenhagen

+45 3527 0540
www.normann-copenhagen.com

and

Nest
+44 (0)114 243 3000
www.nest.co.uk

## One Collection

Ringkøbing, Østergade 11,
DK-6950 Ringkøbing

 +45 7027 7101
www.onecollection.com

and

The Modern Warehouse,
3 Trafalgar Mews, Eastway,
London  E9 5JG

+44 (0)20 8986 0740
www.themodernwarehouse.com

## Rud

Rasmussen, Bredgade 23,
1260 Copenhagen K, Denmark

+45 3539 6233

and

16 Bowling Green Lane,
London  EC1R OBD

+44(0)20 7632 7587
www.rudrasmussen.com

## Sika Design

+45 6615 4224
www.sika-design.com

and

Schiang Living A/S, Albanigade 27,
Odense C 5000, Denmark

 + 45 6612 7035
www.schiang-living.dk

## Snedkergaarden

Snedkergaarden Them A/S,
Knudlundvej 21, Denmark 8653

+45 8684 7799
www.snedkergaarden.com

and

Skandium, 245–9 Brompton Road,
London  SW3 2EP

+44 (0)20 7584 2066
www.skandium.com

# SOURCES

## INTRODUCTION

1 Judith Friedman Hansen, *We are a Little Land: Cultural Assumptions in Danish Everyday Life* (1980), Ayer Company Publishers: Manchester, NH

## HYGGE BY DESIGN

1 *DANISH*<sup>TM</sup>, online magazine promoting Danish architecture and design http://danish.tm/

2 Alain de Botton, *The Architecture of Happiness* (2007), Penguin Books: London

3 Anthony Seldon, *Beyond Happiness: How to find lasting meaning and joy in all that you have* (2015), Yellow Kite: London

4 David Revere McFadden, *Scandinavian Modern Design, 1880–1980* (1982), Harry N. Abrams, Inc.: New York

5 Published to accompany the exhibition 'Scandinavian Moderne 1900–1960', on view October 1997 to September 1998, Wells Fargo Center http://archive.artsmia.org/modernism/e_SM.html

6 Jeppe Trolle Linnet, 'Money Can't Buy Me Hygge: Danish Middle-class Consumption, Egalitarianism, and the Sanctity of Inner Space' (2011)

7 Jeppe Trolle Linnet, 'Cozy Interiority: The Interplay of Materiality and Sociality in the Constitution of Cozy 3rd Place Atmosphere' (2015) http://ambiances.revues.org/543

8 Jonathan Yorke Bean, 'Consuming Hygge at Home: Perception, Representation, Practice' (2011) http://digitalassets.lib.berkeley.edu/etd/ucb/text/Bean_berkeley_0028E_11959.pdf

9 Hansen, *We are a Little Land*

10 De Botton, *The Architecture of Happiness*

11 Linnet, 'Money Can't Buy Me Hygge'

12 Snedkergaarden: +45 8684 7799, snedkergaarden@snedkergaarden.com

## HYGGE LIVING

1 Susan Pinker, *The Village Effect: Why Face-to-Face Contact Matters* (2015), Atlantic Books: London

2 Jonathan Yorke Bean, 'Consuming Hygge at Home: Perception, Representation, Practice' (2011) http://digitalassets.lib.berkeley.edu/etd/ucb/text/Bean_berkeley_0028E_11959.pdf

3 Steven Borish, *The Land of the Living: The Danish Folk High Schools and Denmark's Non-violent Path to Modernization* (2005), Blue Dolphin Publishing: Nevada City

4 *Telegraph*, 12 October 2013: 'How the Great British Bake Off changed Britain' http://www.telegraph.co.uk/foodanddrink/10370144/How-the-Great-British-Bake-Off-changed-Britain.html

5 OECD Obesity Update, June 2014 http://www.oecd.org/health/Obesity-Update-2014.pdf

6 'A Recipe for Inequality', Fabian Commission on Food and Poverty, page 14 http://foodandpoverty.org.uk/wp-content/uploads/2015/03/ARecipefor Inequality_WEB.pdf

7 OECD (2016), Poverty rate (indicator), DOI: 10.1787/0fe1315d-en (accessed 14 June 2016)

8 As reported in the April 2007 edition of *American Psychologist*

9 By permission. http://eating-disorders.org.uk/information/the-psychology -of-dieting/

10 By permission. http://eating-disorders.org.uk/information/the-psychology -of-dieting/

11 World Health Organisation: The European health report 2015 http://www.euro.who.int/en/data-and-evidence/european-health-report/european-health-report-2015/ehr2015

12 Heidi Boye, 'Food and Health in Late Modernity: An Insight into Hygge and Related Food Practices', PhD thesis (2009), Copenhagen Business School http://openarchive.cbs.dk/bitstream/handle/10398/8050/Heidi_Boye.pdf?sequence=1

13 OECD Better Life Index: Work-Life Balance http://www.oecdbetterlifeindex.org/topics/work-life-balance/

14 Meik Wiking, ed., 'The Happy Danes' © Happiness Research Institute 2014

15 OECD Better Life Index: Work-Life Balance http://www.oecdbetterlifeindex.org/topics/work-life-balance/

16  Jeppe Trolle Linnet, 'Money Can't Buy Me Hygge: Danish Middle-class Consumption, Egalitarianism, and the Sanctity of Inner Space' (2011)

17  Bean, 'Consuming Hygge at Home'

18  Statistics Denmark: Denmark in Figures 2016 http://www.dst.dk/Site/Dst/ Udgivelser/GetPubFile.aspx?id=21500&sid=denmark2016

19  *Guardian*, 1 January 2011: 'Is it better to bring up kids in Denmark?' http://www.theguardian.com/lifeandstyle/2011/jan/01/uk-denmark-children -family-swap

20  Linnet, 'Money Can't Buy Me Hygge'

21  Susan Pinker, *The Village Effect: Why Face-to-Face Contact Matters* (2015), Atlantic Books: London, page 8

22  Campaign to End Loneliness: 'Jeremy Hunt highlights loneliness in key speech' http://www.campaigntoendloneliness.org/blog/hunt-highlights-loneliness-2/

23  *Telegraph*, 18 June 2014: 'Britain the loneliness capital of Europe' http://www. telegraph.co.uk/lifestyle/wellbeing/10909524/Britain-the-loneliness-capital- of-Europe.html

24  *The American Spectator*, 18 May 2014: 'The Loneliness of American Society' http://spectator.org/59230_loneliness-american-society/

25  *Guardian*, 20 March 2015: 'Susan Pinker: why face-to-face contact matters in our digital age' https://www.theguardian.com/books/2015/mar/20/ secret-long-happy-life-mountain-villages-sardinia

26  European Social Survey, reference from Wiking, ed., 'The Happy Danes'

27  OECD 'How's Life?' Report 2015 – part of Better Life Initiative https://www. oecd.org/denmark/Better%20Life%20Initiative%20country%20note%20 Denmark.pdf

28  Wiking, ed., 'The Happy Danes'

29  Design Council, 1 June 2014: '5 of the world's most "generous" public spaces' http://www.designcouncil.org.uk/news-opinion/5-world-s-most-generous -public-spaces-wayne-hemingway

30  'A Metropolis for the People', City of Copenhagen (2009) www.kk.dk/ metropolformennesker

31  'A Metropolis for the People', page 7 http://kk.sites.itera.dk/apps/kk_pub2/ pdf/646_mlr0dQ6Wdu.pdf

32  DAC & Cities, 3 February 2014: 'Architectural Policy' http://www.dac.dk/en/ dac-cities/architectural-policy/

33  Quote taken from Gehl Architects website, 2014: 'A people focused national architecture policy' http://gehlarchitects.com/story-article/a-people-focused -national-architecture-policy/

34  Boye, 'Food and Health in Late Modernity'

35  Boye, 'Food and Health in Late Modernity'

36  Boye, 'Food and Health in Late Modernity'

37  Eurostat: 'People in the EU: who are we and how do we live?' 2015 edition http://ec.europa.eu/eurostat/documents/3217494/7089681/KS-04-15-567 -EN-N.pdf/8b2459fe-0e4e-4bb7-bca7-7522999c3bfd

38  See page 6. Published by the City of Copenhagen http://kk.sites.itera.dk/apps/ kk_pub2/pdf/1258_0B5eEF1cF5.pdf

39  Pinker, *The Village Effect*

40  Wiking, ed., 'The Happy Danes', page 50

## HYGGE FOR THE SOUL

1  Darrin M. McMahon, 'From the Happiness of Virtue to the Virtue of Happiness: 400 B.C.–A.D. 1780', *Daedalus* vol. 133, no. 2, 'On Happiness' (spring 2004), pages 5–17, published by The MIT Press on behalf of the American Academy of Arts and Sciences

2  *The Epicurus Reader: Selected Testimonia* (1994), Hackett Publishing Co., Inc.: Cambridge, MA

3  Meik Wiking, ed., 'The Happy Danes' © Happiness Research Institute 2014

4  Wiking, ed., 'The Happy Danes', page 31

5  Wiking, ed., 'The Happy Danes'

6  Helliwell, J., Layard, R., and Sachs, J. (2016). World Happiness Report 2016, Update (vol. I). New York: Sustainable Development Solutions Network

7  Sachs, J., Becchetti, L., & Annett, A. (2016). World Happiness Report 2016, Special Rome Edition (Vol. II). New York: Sustainable Development Solutions Network. World Happiness Report management by Sharon Paculor and Anthony Annett, copy edit by Jill Hamburg Coplan, Aditi Shah and Saloni Jain, design by John Stislow and Stephanie Stislow, cover design by Sunghee Kim. Full text and supporting documentation can be downloaded from the website: http://worldhappiness.report/ ISBN 978-0- 9968513-4-3 Volume II

8  *Journal of Personality and Social Psychology* (American Psychological Association, Inc.), 2001 vol. 80, no. 5: 'Positive Emotions in Early Life and

Longevity: Findings from the Nun Study' https://www.apa.org/pubs/journals/
releases/psp805804.pdf

9  Judith Friedman Hansen, *We are a Little Land: Cultural Assumptions in Danish Everyday Life* (1980), Ayer Company Publishers: Manchester, NH

10  *Guardian*, 3 October 2009: 'This column will change your life: Are some emotions untranslatable?' http://www.theguardian.com/lifeandstyle/2009/oct/03/change-your-life-untranslatable-emotions

11  Breyer, B., and Voss, C. (2016). Happiness and Satisfaction Scale (ISSP). In D. Danner and A. Glöckner-Rist (eds.), Zusammenstellung sozialwissenschaftlicher Items und Skalen. DOI:10.6102/zis240 http://zis.gesis.org/pdf/Dokumentation/Breyer+%20Happiness%20and%20Satisfaction%20Scale%20(ISSP).pdf

12  Eurofound, 9 July 2015: European Quality of Life Survey 2012 http://www.eurofound.europa.eu/surveys/european-quality-of-life-surveys-eqls/european-quality-of-life-survey-2012

13  Heidi Boye, 'Food and Health in Late Modernity: An Insight into Hygge and Related Food Practices', PhD thesis (2009), Copenhagen Business School http://openarchive.cbs.dk/bitstream/handle/10398/8050/Heidi_Boye.pdf?sequence=1

14  Anthony Seldon, *Beyond Happiness: How to find lasting meaning and joy in all that you have* (2015), Yellow Kite: London

15  Jeppe Trolle Linnet, 'Money Can't Buy Me Hygge: Danish Middle-class Consumption, Egalitarianism, and the Sanctity of Inner Space' (2011)

16  *British Medical Journal* 337 DOI: http://dx.doi.org/10.1136/bmj.a2338 (published 05 December 2008). Cited as: BMJ 2008;337:a2338

17  Seldon, *Beyond Happiness*

18  Linnet, 'Money Can't Buy Me Hygge'

19  Boye, 'Food and Health in Late Modernity'

20  Robert Colvile, *The Great Acceleration: How the World is Getting Faster, Faster* (2016) Bloomsbury: London

21  Matthew A. Killingsworth and Daniel T. Gilbert, 'A Wandering Mind Is an Unhappy Mind', http://www.danielgilbert.com/KILLINGSWORTH%20&%20GILBERT%20(2010).pdf

# ACKNOWLEDGEMENTS

Writing a book is a collaborative process, and there are many people I need to thank.

First, my agent, Clare Hulton, and my editor at Trapeze, Anna Valentine, without whose vision, encouragement and gentle guidance it would never have been written at all. That it is a beautiful thing to look at is due to the hard work of the picture and design teams at Trapeze, Emma Smith, Helen Ewing and Debbie Holmes, and the fact that anyone knows it exists is due largely to the efforts of Mark McGinlay. It has been a pleasure working with you all.

I embarked on this project knowing little about either hygge or Denmark, so I am indebted to the many experts who were generous enough to share their knowledge and answer my endless questions; particularly Susanne Nilsson, who patiently explained the basics of hygge grammar, and Jeppe Trolle Linnet, who allowed me access to his illuminating papers. Very many thanks too to Jonathan Yorke Bean, Britta Gertsen, Nicolai de Gier, Thomas Graversen, Sisse Fagt, Knud Erik Hansen, Cecilie Brock Johnsen, Kristina Konsgaard, Tine Mouritsen, Jacob Plejdrup, David Obel Rosenkvist and Meik Wiking, all of whom made time in their overbusy schedules to speak to me.

Writing this book has been all-consuming, and such self-absorption would not have been possible without the understanding and support of my family and friends; I am grateful to you all and can only apologise for my recent neglect.

And finally, thank you, Richard, for cheering me on and, when occasion demanded, reminding me of the bigger picture. I couldn't have got to the end without you.